Praise for
Trusting His Timing

I thoroughly enjoyed reading *Trusting His Timing*. It is the continuation of *Following His Lead*, and I couldn't wait for this one to pick up with the story. It was moving and full of interest and wonder about the characters' lives. It was hard to put the book down until I got to the end. Waiting for the next book!

—Ila Heustess

***

Rhonda Baldwin's second novel, *Trusting His Timing*, is a reminder of God's goodness in both the good times and challenging times of our lives that we all go through! The story is a sequel to her first book, *Following His Lead*. We find out what happens to the two main characters, Cayden and Daniel, that left us with a cliffhanger in her first book. In her second book, we get to know more of the couple's friends, especially Allie and Luke, and really see how their friendships, trials, faith, and trust in God grow deeper as they navigate life! I daresay, we've all been touched by the heartache that Allie experiences in recent years and it's a reminder that God is always in control no matter what man does in this world. I highly recommend *Trusting His Timing*, as you'll see these characters understand that God is always good and His goodness extends to all aspects of our lives, especially during challenging times. Another cliffhanger in book 2? Read for yourself, but I surely can't wait for book 3!

—Robin Kuschel

***

It was a pleasure to be asked to read *Trusting His Timing*! I hope this series continues as I do enjoy reading Rhonda's books. It was very easy for me to get caught up in this story and the characters of this novel. I truly felt as if I was seeing what they were seeing and was praising the Lord right along with them! What a solid testimony these friends have. I found this book very relatable to our current times. I highly recommend this book. What a blessing Rhonda's writing is to me!
—**Cathie Taylor**

***

Trusting His Timing is a wonderful story of a group of friends and family that trust in God's timing. I loved the story and its real-life situations that so many experience. It should remind us that God's timing is always perfect.
—**Theresa Peppell**

***

After waiting for this sequel, I was excited to see what lay ahead for our beloved characters. Having seen them learn to follow, growing in His way, I now got to see them learn to wait on Him in His time, reminding me of my need to trust Him on the seemingly insignificant days to disciple me to trust Him during the most difficult days and months.

We all experienced the COVID pandemic. The characters in *Trusting His Timing* face the same isolation, fear, grief, and loss as we did. They face it all, learning with each trial to trust His will in every part of their journey.

I pray you are blessed and helped as you read their account in *Trusting His Timing*. Truly, they are so us.
—**Cindy Creech**

***

Trusting His Timing, a sequel to Baldwin's first book *Following His Lead,* continues to highlight Cayden's journey as she trusts the Lord's timing in her life.

One of the overall themes is love—romantic, familial, platonic, and, of course, godly (agape). Cayden is inspirational in her acceptance and sharing of God's perfect love. Her motto? "God is good all the time and all the time God is good."

Baldwin's characters are portrayed as "real" flesh and blood people with hopes, dreams, and human frailties, but as they walk in the path of God's love, they remind us that "He hath made every thing beautiful in his time …" (Ecclesiastes 3:11, KJV). An easy read, but one filled with Biblical wisdom and insight.

—**Faith Garbin**, Poet/Playwright

***

Wow! Whether you've read *Following His Lead* or not, you are going to love *Trusting His Timing*! You quickly get invested in the characters and find yourself (depending upon your age) remembering those same kinds of situations. What's going to happen in the end? Who will trust in His timing? It's a great book to curl up on a couch with or to pack when you're heading out on a trip.

—**Renee DiDuro**

Trusting His Timing

Rhonda Baldwin

Published by KHARIS PUBLISHING, an imprint of
KHARIS MEDIA LLC.
Copyright © 2025 Rhonda Baldwin
ISBN 13: 978-1-63746-620-9
ISBN 10: 1-63746-620-X
Library of Congress Control Number:

All KHARIS PUBLISHING products are available at special quantity discounts for bulk purchases for sales promotions, premiums, fund-raising, and educational needs. For details, contact:

Kharis Media LLC
Tel: 1-630-909-3405
support@kharispublishing.com
www.kharispublishing.com

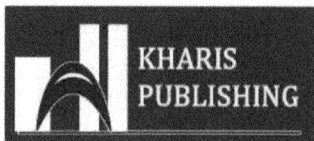

KHARIS
PUBLISHING

Contents

Chapter 1

*A*llie's mom had always told her it was best not to give opinions on a friend's love life, but she couldn't stand around watching her best friend Cayden struggle with frustration and heartache in the romance department and do nothing. So she'd jumped in feet first offering advice but was now beginning to regret not heeding her mother's warning.

They had just left their friend Marta's bridal shower when Cayden pretty much imploded while driving home. Once Allie got her talking, Cayden held nothing back, including her frustration with everyone at the shower asking her who her date for the wedding would be and if she was hearing wedding bells in her immediate future. But Allie knew all the pent-up frustration really stemmed from the uncertainty Cayden felt about their friend Daniel Garrett. Until recently, Daniel had been youth pastor at their church, which meant he worked in the same office with Cayden, who was church secretary. When he accepted a pastor position at another church and they no longer spent time together on a daily basis, their friend/more-than-friend relationship was sort of left in midair. The obvious thing to do was to get Cayden and Daniel talking and all would be well—at least that's what Allie thought until she saw the horrified look that was spreading across Cayden's face as she pushed the End button on her phone. Allie's suggestion that she call Daniel and invite him to be her date for Marta's wedding didn't seem to be working very well.

"Oh no, oh no, oh no!" was all Cayden kept repeating until Allie shook her arm to get her attention.

Not sure what to expect, Allie asked, "What's wrong?" Thinking a little levity would help the matter, she added, "Did you dial the wrong number and invite some other man to be your date?" But her attempt at humor failed dismally, judging by Cayden's expression.

"Do you remember how many times all of us have told Daniel he needs to change his voicemail greeting? Well, he hasn't, and I was so caught up in the moment I didn't give it a thought. When I heard his voice say 'Hi!' I just rattled off 'Daniel, would you like to be my date for Marta's wedding?' As soon as I realized I wasn't actually speaking to Daniel but leaving voicemail, I ended the call. When he listens to the message, he'll probably hear only 'wedding' or 'ding.' What will he think? Oh no, oh no, oh no!" Cayden could only shake her head at the situation she had created.

Trying to make sure she understood Cayden's distress, Allie thought back to exactly what Daniel's voicemail message said. "Oh yeah, we've been telling him now that he's a pastor he should record a more informative, grown-up sounding message. I'm not sure what made him think 'Hi, message please' was a great idea. But Cayden, you know as soon as he sees a missed call from you and then hears whatever your message says, he'll call you back."

Unfortunately, her optimistic take did not seem to help. Cayden was on the verge of tears and Allie was afraid she was going to throw her phone out the car window. Luckily, she was able to convince Cayden to go with her into the restaurant where they had stopped to make the call to freshen up and get something to drink. On their way back to the car, a more composed Cayden asked Allie to drive the last hour home. With a wobbly smile, she laughed at the absurdity of it all and even cracked a small joke. "The one time I decide to ask a guy out, I do it in a voicemail message that makes absolutely no sense! I believe the question of whether or not I have a date for the wedding is settled and that's okay." Looking at Allie and touching her arm to get her attention, she continued, "Thanks for suggesting I do something instead of worrying and sulking. It's so easy for me to forget that God hasn't given me a spirit of fear but of power and love and a sound mind. Right now, I wonder about the *sound mind* part, but making that call was a move toward less fear and more power and that's a move in the right direction."

Realizing a new topic of conversation was needed, they launched into plans to make the next weekend a fun time with their friends. The third member of their best friend trio, Ila Doucet, and her husband, Phillip, would be at Marta's wedding and that meant time to enjoy catching up on what was new in their lives. Phillip and Ila had been married only five months, and most of that time had been spent traveling around the country visiting churches to promote their Feed My Sheep ministry helping homeless people both spiritually and physically. So time with them was precious and just the thing to get their minds looking forward to the wedding festivities.

When Allie pulled up in the driveway at Cayden's apartment and got into her own car to leave, she ventured to give another piece of advice. "Buddy will be waiting for you and that always helps you gain perspective. Take him for a walk, tell him about your day, eat some dinner, and then spend some time with the Lord." Buddy was Cayden's puppy that had found her one day as she was biking in the country. He was great company and, according to Cayden, the best listener. "I'll be expecting a full report on your conversation with Daniel tomorrow morning before Sunday school."

Allie's trip home would take about half an hour, which gave her time to think. It had been only fifteen months since Cayden had come into their lives. After graduation from college, Cayden had spent a week with Marta's family in the mountains of northern Virginia. On her way home to Virginia Beach, her car broke down on I-95 outside of Fredericksburg. Thinking back over the subsequent chain of events, Allie marveled anew at how she could easily see God's hand leading Cayden to her current home and her job at Southside Baptist Church. The tow truck had taken Cayden's car to the garage belonging to Don Mahoney, a fellow Christian and a member of Southside. That connection opened the doors to Cayden becoming church secretary at Southside and best friends with Allie and Ila. It had also resulted in Don and his wife, Beth, renting her a lovely apartment above their detached garage and adopting her as an almost-daughter. Cayden had been a blessing from day one and Allie was grateful God had seen fit to bring her into their lives.

Cayden, Allie, and Ila had become close almost from the start, even though the three girls were quite different in both looks and personality. Cayden was five feet, five inches tall and slender, with auburn hair and blue eyes. She was great at organizing and always ready for the next adventure. Although Ila was about the same height as Cayden, she had a bit more padding in all the right places. Until marrying Phillip, she had been a nurse at the Veterans Health Administration. Ila, who was pretty much the opposite of Allie, had black hair and brown eyes and never met a stranger. Allie was taller with long strawberry blonde hair, and her eyes were a lovely shade of green that changed depending on what she was wearing. Allie preferred to stand in the background and quietly observe and Ila enjoyed being on the front line in order to not miss a thing. Cayden, on the other hand, could lead, follow, or just sit back and take it all in. So different, yet just the right differences to make their friendship strong.

It hadn't taken long before the three were having weekly girls' night dinners. One thing they had in common above all else was their love for the Lord and their desire to follow His will for their lives. That bond made everything else all the sweeter as they spent time together enjoying life and getting to know each other better.

Realizing she was almost home, Allie switched gears and began thinking about her plans for the next two weeks. She had been teaching third grade for three years at the same elementary school she'd attended, and she loved it. Classes would begin in less than a month. She was planning how to decorate her room and updating old lesson plans so that she would be ready to not just teach but mentor the children God and their parents entrusted to her.

As she drove up the lane to her family's farmhouse, she put her window down in order to hear the frogs singing near a pond in the pasture. Her dad and his brother had inherited their parents' five-hundred-acre farm just outside of Ladysmith several years earlier and kept busy managing a thriving business raising and selling livestock and growing corn and soybeans. While Allie enjoyed the larger animals, her favorites were her mom's pygmy goats. One, who had required bottle feeding at birth, had become her pet. He was so small that he would often scoot under the fence, race through their pigpen, and show up at the back door bleating. Because of his love of running through the mud, she named him Pig-Pig, and her mom declared she always knew when Allie was coming up the lane because Pig-Pig would start singing.

Her mom met her at the back door with a hug, while Pig-Pig impatiently butted her leg trying to get her attention. "Hey, boy, wait your turn," she chided before bending down to rub his head right between his little ears. After bringing in her suitcase and giving her mom a quick rundown on her trip, she went back out with an apple and settled in to pay the little goat some attention. Once again, it struck her how much she loved her home and her family. Sending a quick thanks up to God for the many blessings He bestowed on her every day, she went back inside to help with dinner and settle in for a quiet Saturday night.

Meanwhile, Cayden was waiting for her phone to ring. She agreed with Allie that Daniel would see the missed call, listen to the odd voicemail, and call her back. After fixing a light supper and taking Buddy out for a short walk, she tried to study her lesson for the Sunday school class she would be teaching the next morning. However, her mind kept going back to Daniel and her heart started fretting over the whole situation. Time and time again, she had turned it over to the Lord and each time she took it back. As she tried to pray, something from a lesson their study group had discussed the previous week nudged at the edges of her misery. The Bible study author, Cynthia Heald, had talked about the importance of sitting quietly at the feet of Jesus, not asking for anything or pouring your heart out, just quietly waiting and listening with an open heart.

After putting Buddy in his crate for the night, Cayden tearfully asked the Lord to forgive her for choosing to fret and letting fear take hold in her heart. She quoted her favorite verse, Jeremiah 29:11 (KJV) "For I know the thoughts that I think toward you, saith the Lord, thoughts of peace, and not of evil, to give you an expected end," thanked Him for loving her, and then sat quietly. The earth didn't shake and the world kept spinning as usual, but Cayden's open heart was flooded with a sweet peace and joy that overflowed in tears as the Holy Spirit comforted her with words of assurance and love. With a calm beyond her understanding and knowledge that her Heavenly Father had everything under control according to *His* plan for her life, she went to bed and slept peacefully.

The next morning, Allie didn't get a chance to catch up with Cayden until they were in the choir practice room after Sunday school. She was excited to hear how the conversation between Daniel and Cayden had gone the night before. However, her excitement turned to total dismay when Cayden said he hadn't called.

"What do you mean he didn't call?" she almost shouted. Realizing others might hear, she lowered her voice and motioned Cayden to follow her to an empty classroom. "Are you sure he didn't call while you were out with Buddy or showering? I mean there's no way he wouldn't call you back."

"Believe me I checked my phone all evening, but no call," was all Cayden had to say. But her calm demeanor and slight smile were Allie's undoing.

"Well, it just doesn't make sense, just like it doesn't make sense that you're all calm and happy. Why am I more aggravated with Daniel than you are?" Allie's ire had cooled a bit and Cayden's calm took the wind out of her angry sails, but not totally. "I'm going to call him as soon as church is over and get to the bottom of this!"

Before she could go on, Cayden touched her hand, thanked her for being such a wonderful friend, and then told her not to call him. Allie opened her mouth to respond just as the choir director started practice for the morning choir special. She gave up for the time being, but her irritation with Daniel hadn't totally dissipated.

After church, the girls had no time to talk. Allie's mom was hosting Sunday dinner at the farm for the family and several out-of-town friends, which meant racing home to finish last-minute preparations. Cayden was glad because she wanted to just relish the joy and peace that had come from her time with God. She didn't know how it would all work out, but she was happy to rest knowing He had a plan, it was for her good, and it would be His timing—not hers.

After choir practice that evening, Allie tried to corner Cayden and get some answers, but Pastor Harwell needed help with something in the office that kept Cayden busy until time for evening service to begin. However, she was not going to let this go. Although she might be the quietest one of their group, she couldn't stand by when a friend was hurting and not try to help. Daniel needed to understand how rude it was not to return Cayden's call, and Cayden just had to give her the green light to give Daniel a piece of her mind.

As the first song was announced and they stood to sing, Cayden felt a funny sensation on her neck, like when someone softly breathes on your skin. Turning around to see who might be behind her, she saw Daniel at the back of the church talking with Pastor. The sensation she'd felt earlier was nothing compared to the sweet feeling that flooded over her as Daniel looked her way and smiled. Nothing in her life had ever been clearer or more certain than the thought and feeling that welled up in her heart. At that moment, Cayden realized that she was looking at the man she loved.

Allie's nudge brought Cayden back to the song service and she turned around, joining in the singing. How appropriate, they were singing "Jesus, Jesus, Jesus, sweetest name I know." Jesus was indeed her heart's melody, but he had added another sweet, new melody in her heart concerning Daniel, and her peace was one hundred percent as she accepted its truth. She was in love with Daniel Garrett.

Services commenced and several times Cayden could feel Allie gazing at her with a quizzical look. Wanting to enjoy Pastor's sermon, she chose to resist looking back at her in case Allie could somehow discern what had happened. Sometimes, it was just nice to hold sweet feelings close to your own heart for a while and enjoy the wonder without having to answer anyone else's questions.

After church, their friend Luke and Daniel asked them if they wanted to go to Olaf's. Their old group, which had also included Phillip and Ila, had made a habit of visiting their favorite restaurant after services on a fairly regular basis. They had already invited the new youth pastor, Simon Peter

Walker, and his wife, Coral, to join them. When Daniel mentioned it to Allie, she gave him the cold shoulder and waited to hear Cayden's response. Not wanting to cause a scene right there in church, Allie liked the idea of confronting Daniel about his rude behavior when they got to Olaf's. So when Cayden agreed to go, she let them know she'd join them too.

Cayden suggested she and Allie ride together in order to give her time to reiterate that Allie was not to ask Daniel about not returning her call. It was strange when the usually quiet, docile Allie got her back up, but they all knew when that happened she could be a force to be reckoned with. Cayden's new peace and trust in God's planning would have to rub off on Allie really quickly as they only had a few miles to go before arriving at the restaurant. However, as it turned out, Coral also asked to ride with them to give the three young women time to catch up. That meant Allie was still simmering when the group sat down at their table.

As soon as Olaf saw them come in, he immediately came over to welcome them personally. Earlier that year, Olaf had asked Phillip why their group was so different, which opened the door for Phillip to explain and lead Olaf to the Lord. Since that time, he had shared his testimony with anyone who listened, and many had come to know Jesus because of his excitement in telling them how God had saved him.

After the waiter had taken their orders, Allie was ready to talk to Daniel. She had purposely sat next to him so they could talk without everyone being part of the conversation. Just as she was about to speak, Luke asked Daniel why he hadn't returned his call from Saturday morning.

"You said you'd like to play in the academy's golf tournament, and I needed to see if you were interested in order to get a team together. Tomorrow's the last day to register. Interested?" Like Allie, Luke was a school teacher but at a Christian academy in Fredericksburg.

"Sorry, but I didn't know you'd called. My phone has literally died." After taking a sip of coffee, he explained further. "Some of the guys from church invited me to go fishing on the bay yesterday and, of course, I jumped at the chance. I mean fishing and getting to know my flock at the same time— that's just perfect. It wasn't until I got back to the Jeep that I realized my phone was dead. Even after I plugged it in, it just wouldn't turn on. Of course, it was too late to go to the store last night. Then, today, we had two missionaries visiting. Remember Larry Harrison, serving in Mexico? He spoke in the morning, and what a great service. Afterward, we had a covered-dish dinner, followed by an update and sermon from one of our new missionaries.

That was in lieu of a service tonight, which is why I was able to make it to Southside pretty much on time."

As he was speaking, Allie looked over at Cayden, who was sitting quietly with a peaceful, contented look on her face. Catching her eye, she mouthed "Sorry" to her best friend. Daniel had a good reason not to call Cayden, and Allie hadn't been ready to wait and see before wanting to pounce on him. With her usual sunny disposition restored, Allie realized she would use that whole experience to teach her third graders not to jump to conclusions and waste time and emotions before even knowing the facts.

Talk turned to plans for the coming week. Just as Cayden was about to mention Marta's wedding, Daniel spoke up. "Hey, Cayden, is Saturday Marta and Wade's big day? Oh, yeah, how was the bridal shower yesterday? I know you were looking forward to it."

"The shower was lovely. It was nice to reconnect with lots of Marta's family and some of our college friends." Cayden responded without even thinking about the drama over a date for the wedding. It had worked out the way it should, and she was glad. She was also happy Daniel remembered something important happening in her life. That was nice.

Allie chimed in with her account of the shower and their plans for the wedding weekend. "I'm going up with Cayden on Friday. Even though I'm not part of the wedding party, Marta insisted I attend the rehearsal dinner. After hearing the menu, which consists of lots of authentic Mexican dishes, I was more than happy to accept."

Luke asked, "Will Ila be able to come for the wedding? I never can keep track of where their ministry takes them these days."

Agreeing wholeheartedly, Allie responded, "I try to keep up with their travels, but it's not easy. They're planning on attending the wedding, and I'm really looking forward to catching up with them. I didn't realize how much I'd miss Ila!" As an afterthought, she quickly added, "And Phillip too, of course," which made everyone laugh.

Talk continued until Simon volunteered to pray for all of them as they started a new week and everyone went their separate ways. As they left the restaurant, Daniel walked with Cayden and Allie, chatting about a church picnic the next Saturday. Looking at Cayden, he said, "I had hoped you might like to come to our church picnic with me next weekend, but then I recalled the date of the wedding and knew it wouldn't be possible. Maybe next time."

"I would have loved that. It would have given me a chance to put names with faces. Definitely next time." Getting in her car, Cayden smiled and told him good night. Allie heard a soft sigh as Cayden put the car in gear and backed out of the parking spot.

Glad to finally have Cayden to herself in order to ask some very important questions, Allie didn't waste any time. "Did that sigh I just heard have anything to do with the goofy look you had during church?"

Caught a bit off guard, Cayden sputtered, "What do you mean a goofy look? I didn't have any more of a goofy look than usual!" Realizing how that sounded, they both burst into laughter. By the time they had calmed down, they were pulling into the church parking lot. "Allie, all kidding aside, thank you for not lighting into Daniel about not calling. He had a great reason, but even if he just didn't think to return my call, it really was still quite all right."

Not ready to put all this to rest, Allie advised Cayden to park the car and put the windows down. "We have some talking to do, and I'm not budging from your car until I have some answers."

Laughing, Cayden did as she was told and parked beside Allie's car. "Okay, shoot. I'll answer your questions if I know the answer."

"Let's start with this morning. I was fit to be tied when you said Daniel didn't call you back, but you were all mellow and peaceful. To be honest, it was a bit irritating because you should have been more put out than I was." Allie had to stop and regroup, which gave Cayden time to interject.

"I don't know if anger ever came into play, but I was hurt and not just by Daniel's supposed lack of consideration. I was hurt that God wasn't working like I thought He should be. Then the Holy Spirit reminded me of something we discussed last week in our Bible study. Remember how in the *Becoming a Woman of Excellence* lesson Mrs. Heald explained the need for us to sit at Jesus's feet and quietly wait on Him?" Cayden stopped to get a tissue out of her purse before continuing. "Allie, I realized I've never done that. I'm always busy doing, thinking, planning—so busy I think I often miss hearing His voice speaking to me."

Totally mesmerized by the conversation, Allie could only murmur, "Don't stop now. What happened?"

"Well, I'm sorry to say that it took me truly being at my wit's end before I did as Mrs. Heald suggested. I asked Jesus to forgive my fears and frustrations and then sat quietly, waiting with my heart open. The Cayden you saw this morning and are seeing now is a woman at peace with God and with herself. I know that God's plan for me doesn't hinge on things going a certain way I think they should go and that I am to relax knowing He is in control instead of constantly struggling." Realizing that about summed it up, Cayden grew quiet.

More than satisfied with her friend's answer, Allie continued with her questions. "Okay, that explains this morning and your calm demeanor. In fact, I'll go so far as to add that you seem downright joyful." Seeing Cayden nod in agreement, she went on, "So what was up with the goofy face during church tonight? I mean, I've known you for a while now and have never seen you look like that before. What was that about?"

Unable to contain her excitement and joy, Cayden told her about turning around to see Daniel and the realization that dawned on her. "As clear as day, when Daniel looked at me and smiled, my heart was filled with the absolute knowledge that I was looking at the man I love."

Now, it was Allie's turn to be awestruck, and she just sat there with a very odd look on her face, unable to respond. Cayden laughed so hard she could hardly breathe, and when she'd caught her breath, she said, "Now who's the one with a goofy look on her face?"

After a bit more conversation and a quick prayer of joyful thankfulness and anticipation of what God was working in their lives, Allie got in her car and they left the parking lot. Her ride home was different from the ride the day before. This time, she was full of praise and glory for Her Lord and the wonderful blessings He lavishly bestows. Watching Ila and Phillip fall in love had been fun and a whirlwind, but she couldn't wait to watch this wonderful romance between Cayden and Daniel blossom and grow. As she drove up their driveway, she offered a final praise, "God is good all the time and all the time God is good! Thank you, Jesus!"

Monday evening, Cayden was cleaning up after dinner when Buddy started whining and running for the door. That had to mean someone was coming up the stairs to her apartment. By the time she reached the door, he was excitedly barking and jumping up and down, which was a sign he recognized the footsteps as someone he liked a lot. Thinking it must be Don or Beth, she opened the door, laughing at the little dog's antics, and was surprised to see Daniel on the landing instead.

Catching her breath, all she could think to say was, "Well, I wasn't expecting you." Even to her foggy brain, which was brought on by seeing Daniel, that sounded terribly inhospitable. So she quickly invited him in. He scooped Buddy up and came in, all the while dodging sloppy puppy kisses.

Amid Cayden scolding Buddy for bad manners, Daniel let her know it was quite all right. "He's okay. I enjoy it. Sometimes, it's nice to see unfettered enthusiasm and undisguised love." Going into the living room, they sat on the sofa with Buddy jumping happily between two of his most loved people.

After the usual pleasantries, Daniel explained his visit. "First, sorry I didn't call before dropping by, which would have been polite. I just left the cell phone store and checked my messages from the last few days. When I saw you'd called and heard your very short, somewhat cryptic message, I decided to come on over. I hope you don't mind."

Noticing his look of embarrassment, she was quick to assure him it was fine. In her heart, she was thinking how much more than fine it was to see him and to know how quickly he wanted to respond to her call on Saturday. She and Allie had been right—he would have called if he'd known she had called him.

"I'm glad I saw you last night and knew you were all right or I would have been concerned something was wrong. Want to fill me in on your message?" He played it for her and, sure enough, it pretty much consisted of only the word "wedding."

Surprised that she wasn't in the least flustered at having to now explain everything, she thanked the Holy Spirit for the calm He provided and then suggested that they take Buddy for a walk. It was time she and Daniel talked to each other instead of other people, and her heart was ready to see what happened next.

As they walked toward the street with Buddy leading the way, they chatted for a few minutes about how big Buddy was getting and how their days had gone before Daniel asked again, "Your message mentioned something about a wedding. I'm guessing you were talking about Marta's wedding, right?"

Relieved that none of this felt awkward, Cayden filled him in on the reason for her Saturday call and her odd message. "I thought you might like to go to the wedding with me." Lightly punching his arm, she continued, "Sorry the message was confusing, but that's not all my fault, you know. Your voicemail greeting makes a person think they're actually talking to you, especially if they're already flustered."

"In my defense, I have been a bit busy lately, but you're right. One of the men at church mentioned the same thing recently. I promise to change it as soon as I get home this evening." Unable to resist, he innocently asked, "So you were flustered when you called to ask me to go to the wedding with you? Why would that be?"

"Because the whole message went something like this, 'Daniel, would you like to be my date for Marta's wedding?' and asking a guy to be my date isn't something I'd ever done before." Glad that was over, she sighed before stopping and looking directly at him. "What would you have said if you didn't have a church picnic on the same day?"

"I would have asked what time I should be there and the address," he replied without hesitation. "If I wasn't new to the church, I might have considered missing the picnic just to be your date, but it might look a bit odd for the new pastor to skip a function where he can meet and fellowship with the people he's been called to shepherd. But just because I'm not free for the wedding doesn't mean we can't plan something else. Would that be something you'd like?"

And just like that, there they were—walking along a country road with a little dog they'd rescued together about to start a conversation that could change their lives. Yet neither of them seemed afraid or worried. In fact, anyone passing by would see two young people with matching expressions of hope and joy. Finally, it was time.

"Yes, Daniel, I believe I'd like that very much," she replied as she looked up into his eyes just as his cell phone rang. Seeing him struggle with whether to answer or not, she grinned and said, "Important men receive important calls. Go ahead and take it."

When he caught up with her and Buddy, he explained that he had a meeting with the deacons at eight. "I hate to cut our walk short, but we need to head back. So about that date, would Thursday night for dinner work? I don't want to wait until after you get back from the wedding. Thursday good for you?"

An agreement was reached for him to pick Cayden up at six Thursday night. He would take care of reservations, and they could talk about anything else when he called her at noon the next day. As he was leaving, he gave her a wide smile and said, "I've missed you," to which she replied, "Same!"

Chapter 2

Meanwhile, back at the farm, Allie was telling her mom about how her day had gone. With just a few days before the children returned to the classroom, teachers were busy with lesson plans, decorating their rooms, and settling in for another year of sharing themselves and their knowledge with little people who needed what they had to give. Everyone enjoyed catching up with what had been happening during the summer and meeting any new staff. The afternoon was set aside for a staff meeting where the principal updated them on anything new for the year and the safety officer did her annual review and highlighted any changes, along with CPR recertification.

Allie was excited about the last agenda item, the religious education classes held every Tuesday. Her mom and a few other teachers had worked hard to get the classes approved years earlier and the children enjoyed them, as did the teachers. Children whose parents signed permission slips attended the class in the lunchroom, while the few remaining students were given a fun assignment. One teacher from each grade would have those children in a classroom, giving the other teachers a chance for a bit of catch-up or for a quick cup of coffee with no disruption. The younger children attended a class in the morning, and the older children attended an afternoon class. It all worked well and over the years hadn't run into any real opposition. That is until the end of the staff meeting when the principal turned the meeting over to Allie as this year's sponsor teacher to discuss plans and Elizabeth Zenna-Parlieu raised her hand to speak.

Elizabeth had joined the third-grade teacher staff two years earlier. Liz, as her friends called her, kept pretty much to herself and seemed to love her students. However, the only time Allie had seen her be friendly to anyone was with the children. She isolated herself even when Allie and some of the others invited her to go out to eat or to ride to a conference with them. It appeared she preferred her own company and, after a while, it was easier to accept her wishes and just be kind and cordial with her but nothing more.

Hoping that Elizabeth finally wanted to be a part of the program and offer assistance, Allie welcomed her to speak. It took only a minute for everyone to realize Elizabeth wasn't offering help but was extremely opposed to this or any other type of religious program in the school.

"When I started teaching here two years ago, I was surprised such a program is allowed in a public school, but being new I kept my mouth shut. Last year, it became evident that the program also causes scheduling and logistics problems for us teachers, not to mention disruption for the children." As Elizabeth continued speaking, her voice began to rise slightly and she became more animated, shaking her head and motioning with her hands. Allie could tell she was serious and couldn't understand her apparent anger concerning the program, but she did realize it was time to get the meeting back on track. However, before she could say anything, Elizabeth continued. "Over the summer, I've talked with some parents who also have questions concerning the program and we plan to meet with the school superintendent."

Before Elizabeth could continue, Allie spoke up, "Thank you, Liz, for voicing your concerns. We like to work as a team, so it's important that we're all on the same page. I'm just sorry you didn't feel you could talk with anyone on our school staff in order to give us a chance to explain how the program came about and the benefit it has for the students."

"Excuse me, my name is Elizabeth and I wasn't quite finished," Elizabeth frostily declared, quickly putting Allie definitely in the not-my-friend zone. "I would like to ask that the weekly classes be postponed until the superintendent reviews the situation and makes a determination." She sat down, staring straight ahead, waiting for her request to be addressed.

Allie didn't miss a beat in replying, "This program was implemented many years ago and has been good for our students. I have to, therefore, respectfully deny your request. In order to be sure Superintendent Barker understands the program and how it's run, I'll be joining you at the meeting. When is the appointment, please?"

Getting to her feet and picking up her things, Elizabeth began to leave the room before turning to say, "I can't stop you from being there, but you can find out the details for yourself."

A stunned silence filled the room as teachers and aides looked at each other, wondering what in the world had just happened. Allie assured them she would find out the date and time of the meeting and let them all know. She couldn't help but think it looked like this was going to be an interesting and, perhaps, challenging year and that Elizabeth didn't know who she was up against. While the teachers were upset and perhaps angry, Allie wasn't talking about them. She meant God. The religious classes belonged to Him and Elizabeth was no match for Him.

Allie's mother Rae knew something was wrong as soon as her daughter got out of the car and started walking to the back door. Her step, usually so light and quick, was heavy and slow. Even Pig-Pig knew something was off because he walked gently beside her instead of butting her knees with his head and crying for attention. Something had to have happened to get her sunshine girl down, which caused Rae to stop and send up a quick prayer before calling out a sweet welcome.

As Allie filled Rae in on the meeting and Elizabeth's remarks, she found herself getting angry at the other woman for being so unreasonable and unfriendly. Finding it rather enjoyable to go with the anger for a few minutes, she thought of ways she should have stopped Elizabeth in her tracks and shut her down with some quick, cutting remarks. Just who did she think she was to cause problems in *her* school? Then she plainly heard a familiar voice in her heart reminding her to love her neighbor, who in this case was Elizabeth, and a sadness filled her for the woman in question.

Laying her head on her mom's shoulder, she let go of the tears that had threatened to choke her on the way home. Giving Allie a minute to relax, Rae just hugged her close before speaking. "Are you crying because you're mad or frustrated or because you sensed something under Elizabeth's cold demeanor that touched your heart?" Trying to lighten the mood, she added, "You and Pig-Pig have that in common, you know. Maybe it's a goat-sense type of thing where you feel another person's or goat's pain." She could tell when her daughter's mood changed and knew it was okay to proceed. "From what you've told me about Elizabeth, and that hasn't been much, I gathered you think she's hurting in some way. Could all of this stem from whatever may be causing her pain?"

As she wiped away tears, Allie took out two glasses and filled them with iced tea, setting one in front of her mother before sitting down at the kitchen island. "Just this morning, as I was finishing up my devotions and praying, the Lord brought Liz—I mean Elizabeth—to mind and I prayed for her. She just won't let me get close enough to know if she's married or has children, likes cats or hates dogs, or even where she's from. Some of the other teachers have said pretty much the same thing and we all agree if she wants to be left alone, we can oblige. But this morning I knew I was supposed to pray and it happened again right before the staff meeting, so I prayed for her a second time."

Jumping up to check a cake in the oven and stir the crockpot, Rae looked back at Allie and assured her that she would join in praying. Then the two Lambert ladies began to put their heads together to come up with a plan for making sure the religious education classes would continue. When it was time to meet with Superintendent Barker, Allie would be ready to defend the program and the need of it for the children in their school.

A farm can be a hard place to be alone. Oh, people might not be around, but there are always animals that want to tag along or be petted. So when Allie changed clothes and headed out the back door for a walk, she was joined by not only Pig-Pig but also two barn cats. But she couldn't complain as she meandered down the path to the hay barn. At least they couldn't talk or have an opinion, and their company was a good distraction. When they were kids, her father had hung two rope swings from a large oak tree near the barn to entertain them while he worked nearby. Without thinking, she sat down and started slowly swinging back and forth, feeling her emotions subside with each push of her feet. Her mom was right. She had always felt that Elizabeth was hurt and sad but she'd never been able to talk to her long enough to get a handle on what was wrong or how to help her. Now it seemed that might never happen if they wound up on opposite sides of a topic that could push a lot of emotional buttons for many people.

Dinner at the farm was always a time for the family to catch up over Rae's good home cooking. Richard, Allie's dad, would fill them in on what was happening around the farm and any local news. Her oldest brother, Gil, always had funny stories from his job as a lineman for the cable company. While he had built a nice, brick house on acreage their parents had given him, he almost always came "home" for dinner. Joey, Allie's senior by two years, still lived at home and had equally entertaining anecdotes from his day working as a carpenter for a local builder. Allie's tales from school almost always brought laughter. Rae pretty much just took it all in and thanked the Lord for this time she had with her children.

A walk, dinner, and a nice, long shower had bolstered Allie's spirits and she decided to call Cayden as she settled in for the evening. After the usual pleasantries, she told Cayden about the situation with Elizabeth and asked her to pray about the upcoming meeting but, more importantly, to pray for her to know how to talk and perhaps befriend someone who didn't seem at all keen to make friends.

"Oh, Allie, you know I'll be praying. It's hard when you'd like to help a person and they only want to be left alone or sometimes even forgotten. It almost seems like Elizabeth has been in the 'leave me alone' mindset but is now pushing against that. Maybe it's a sign she wants to connect but is just going about it in a terribly wrong way." Cayden paused as if to figure out a better way to say what she was thinking. "If all she wants is to be forgotten and left alone, then why pick a fight? Why not continue flying under the radar like she's done for the last two years? From what you've said, there's nothing new with the program, which may mean there is something new with her."

"Golly, Cayden, I hadn't given that a thought. Do you think there's something in her life that might have caused her to want to be left alone and now she's tired of it and wants to be a part of things again?" Even thinking that might be the case made Allie's heart ache for Elizabeth. Somehow, she would have to find out more about this person who was suddenly on the forefront of her mind. "Thanks for praying. I'll have to text Ila and ask her to pray with us too."

"I'll tell Daniel about the situation and you know he'll be praying," Cayden interjected. "In fact, he lives in that area and may even know Elizabeth. Wouldn't that be something?"

Before Cayden could go on, Allie almost shouted, "Whoa! Whoa! Whoa! What do you mean you'll tell Daniel? Since when are you just happening to be talking to Daniel? Girl, you better fill me in if something's changed!"

Happy to oblige, Cayden told Allie how Daniel had come by and they'd talked and walked and were going out to dinner Thursday night. She expected what came next and wasn't disappointed when Allie started hollering, "Praise the Lord! Finally! Thank you, Jesus!"

After Allie was satisfied Cayden had told her everything, she prayed a prayer of thanks and guidance for Daniel and Cayden. As she was about to say "Amen," Cayden picked up the prayer asking the Lord to help Allie know how to help Elizabeth and how best to handle the meeting with Superintendent Barker.

As Allie turned out the light and started to get into bed, she remembered Cayden's reminder that all Jesus wanted was for her to trust Him in the good times and the bad. She didn't have to know all the answers and be ready to fight the battle alone. After asking God to forgive her earlier attitude, she bowed her head and silently waited—not asking for anything or even thanking Him for all the blessings in her life—just waiting to hear from her Heavenly Father. As she waited, a sweet peace filled her heart and soul, and she was assured that God would work it all out for His glory. When she finally climbed into bed, it was with the precious knowledge that God was in control, and He would lead her in how to walk through this particular valley. She fell asleep praising the Lord and was ready to face tomorrow.

The rest of the week seemed to fly by for both Cayden and Allie. Cayden was looking forward to her first official date with Daniel and Allie was busy with last-minute preparations for the first day of school. Plans for the upcoming wedding weekend were in place, which worked out well since they were so busy they had no time to talk until early Thursday morning.

Allie was the first to bring up Cayden's date. "So where is Daniel taking you for dinner tonight? He did call you like he promised, right?" she asked jokingly.

"Not only has he called, but he's sent flowers and texts," Cayden replied smugly. "But he won't tell me where we're going. He just said to dress casually, which left me sorting through my closet last night. I finally chose my yellow sleeveless dress with the cute blue sweater. Not to change the subject, but how did your day go? Any more from Liz?"

Allie took a moment before responding, "I didn't even set eyes on her today, which must mean her room's all ready for the big day. I did poke my head in and take a peek. If her classroom reflects the 'real' Elizabeth, then she has a really sweet, thoughtful heart. Her students will feel like they're being hugged when they walk in the door with her choice of colors and fun decorations. The woman is such an enigma."

Talk continued for just a few minutes when they had to go in order to start their workdays. Each promised to pray for the other, and the next morning they would have at least two hours on the road to Winchester to discuss everything.

Cayden was the only one in the church office until lunchtime when Simon returned from a local Bible conference he and Pastor attended that morning. That had given her time to get a lot of work done before being off the next day for the wedding. As Simon started into his office, he quickly turned and walked back to her desk. Smiling, he said, "Coral reminded me that tonight's the big night. First dates are exciting but can be a little unnerving."

Seeing she was beginning to look a bit anxious all of a sudden, he added something that might help. "Here's a bit of good news. Pastor told me to tell you to take the afternoon off to give you extra time to get ready for your weekend trip." When Cayden didn't start moving, he added, "A little birdy may or may not have told him about tonight, which means that might or might not have factored in his generous offer. Either way, you need to shut down your computer, grab your purse, and get out of here!"

At six on the dot, Buddy scrambled off his favorite seat on the couch and scurried to the door whining. Although he was a little pup, he was a great alarm system. When Daniel knocked on the door, Buddy launched into his big-dog barking routine that fooled no one but seemed to make him happy. Cayden knew that when she opened the door, he would be more than excited to see Daniel and the fun would really begin. He would run into the bedroom, grab his favorite hedgehog toy, and drop it at Daniel's feet, knowing a game of fetch would surely ensue. After a few minutes of running back and forth, he would roll over onto his back and expect his belly to be scratched, after which he would gladly climb onto the nearest lap and settle in for a short nap. As usual, Daniel did exactly as Buddy expected with the end result that Cayden expected—a happy but tired puppy.

Relieved that Daniel was dressed in khakis and a polo shirt, Cayden felt she was dressed appropriately for the evening and decided to relax and enjoy their time together. It was going to be interesting to see how the transition from coworkers/friends to possible boyfriend and girlfriend would work. Knowing how many people were praying for them made relaxing easier. Add to that the fact that Buddy had already put his seal of approval on the evening, what more could they want?

As they walked to Daniel's Jeep, Cayden knew at least two sets of eyes were watching their progress from the house. She had seen a familiar car in the driveway when she got home, which meant Ellen Garver was visiting with Beth. Ellen was Beth's best friend and one of Cayden's oldest friends in Fredericksburg. Coincidence? Not likely!

Don, on the other hand, had decided the direct approach was better. He came out of the garage and spoke directly to Daniel, "Young man, as a stand-in for Cayden's father, I have a few questions for you."

Daniel blinked a couple of times before responding. "Yes, sir. I thought that might be the case. We're going to dinner and then possibly for a short walk before I bring her home. She has a lot going on the next few days so I promise to get her home before ten. Does that meet with your approval?"

"I guess that will do since I know you're an honorable, godly man. Just don't be surprised if I'm still out here working at ten." Don's expression never changed as he looked Daniel in the eyes without even a trace of a smile on his face. Then he looked at Cayden and winked before walking back inside and closing the door behind him.

"Golly!" was all Daniel could say. He'd known Don for several years and seen him serious and jovial, but this was a new side of him. Cayden could only laugh since she knew he had not seen Don wink at her. Their date was off to a great start!

Still not knowing where he was taking her for dinner, Cayden started asking questions to which Daniel would only say, "Just be patient." Knowing patience was not something she was known for, Daniel enjoyed spinning the intrigue. As he drove south out of Fredericksburg, her mind began flitting through the restaurant choices in a radius that would allow them time to eat, take a walk, and get back to her apartment by ten. Soon a satisfied grin broke across her face, which made Daniel wonder if she had guessed their destination.

"You think you've got it nailed down, don't you?" he asked, giving her a questioning glance.

Playing along, she only smiled. After all, two could play at this game.

They settled into easy conversation about their day and news from their friends. Several minutes later, they arrived at a familiar restaurant and Cayden couldn't help exclaiming, "I knew it! As soon as you turned a few miles back, I guessed we were coming here."

"This is the first place we shared a meal together. Remember? You came in after church that Sunday morning and I was sitting at my reserved table. When you saw there was a waiting line, you were going to leave until I asked if you wanted to join me." As he spoke, Daniel recalled how he thought even then that he might be in trouble where this beautiful woman was concerned.

Smiling at the memory, Cayden replied, "Yep, I couldn't understand how you'd already made it from church to the restaurant and were sitting at a table. That is until I saw the 'reserved' sign on your table, but that still baffled me in a small diner. Then you shared the secret. Your cousin is the owner and always saves you a table on Sundays just in case you might show up. How's he doing?"

"Still going strong and still saving my corner table, which really comes in handy now that I'm a pastor and preaching Sunday mornings and evenings.

It's a bit closer to my new church, and I come here a lot to eat and then get home for some rest and study before returning for evening service. By the way, he has homemade peach ice cream on the dessert menu. In fact, he has it especially for you." Seeing the startled look on her face, he was satisfied once again that he'd thought to ask his cousin for this favor.

"How lovely! I'll have to thank him and I think I should thank you also for remembering that peach is my favorite flavor," she said as they were seated at the corner table decorated with a lovely floral arrangement. Looking around, she realized that no other tables were adorned with flowers and surmised this special touch must have been Daniel's doing. He really was going all out and she loved it.

The evening progressed with easy conversation and a delicious meal. Daniel's cousin stopped by to say hello, remind them of peach ice cream waiting in the freezer, and place a gift bag beside Daniel before returning to the kitchen. Intrigued, Cayden waited patiently to see what came next.

"I have a special gift for you," he said as he handed her the bag. "It's long overdue and I thought this was the perfect time to set some things right." As she took the bag, he continued, "That first day I met you, I acted like a tongue-tied teenager and didn't make the best impression. Pastor had told me about his new secretary, but he didn't mention she was a beautiful young woman with auburn hair, blue eyes, long lashes, and adorable freckles. That's what I saw when I bounded into the office that morning expecting to meet a woman my mom's age."

By that time, Cayden was smiling, really enjoying this bit of wonderful information. "Ah, yes, that first day was quite interesting. I recall a remark about my expensive coffee and how that money could have helped missions and then something about you 'borrowing' money from the coffee fund in order to buy a Peppermint Patty to apologize, which backfired when I walked in on you taking the change out of the till. But all was well when you explained, took your own money, and presented me with that lovely peace offering."

"Well, I was glad you accepted my apology and forgave me. Now, whenever I see a Peppermint Patty, I smile and think of you." Handing her the bag, he explained, "This is to commemorate that day and to say thank you for forgiving me and giving me another chance."

When Cayden opened the bag and found dozens of the silver-wrapped candy in differing sizes, she laughed and reached over to take his hand. They had come so far since that first meeting. Far enough, in fact, for her to understand that this gesture meant a lot. Although there would surely be more times they didn't see eye-to-eye or totally get what the other was thinking, there would always be a way to work through it and find a way to forgive and go on. Who knew a piece of candy could be so powerful?

After dinner, they drove to a nearby park for a leisurely stroll. As they walked along listening to the night sounds and enjoying the cooler evening air, she stumbled on a tree root and he grabbed her hand to steady her. Thinking it felt just right, he kept her hand in his as they continued walking and talking.

"After that first meeting, who would have guessed we'd eventually be dating? And I say 'eventually' because you have to admit it took us a while to get here. Right?" Daniel stopped to look at her as she began to reply.

"Well, you've been honest about that first day and I'll be honest too." Cayden smiled at him and continued. "I was in this great new job and really wanted to succeed, which meant my concern was how you would fit into that. Since you owned up to acting like a teenager, I feel it's okay to share with you that I went home that day thinking I didn't need another pesky brother and just hoped we could work well together." Seeing his eyes widen at this last remark, she hurried to add, "But it didn't take long to realize we could be not only coworkers but also friends, and that's been wonderful."

Guiding her over to a bench to sit down, Daniel was quiet for a few seconds before bursting into laughter. "So since we're on our first date, I take it I made it past the pesky brother status. How cool is that? I can't wait to tell my sisters. They won't believe it!"

As she sighed with relief that her revelation hadn't upset him, she assured him, "If they don't believe you, just give them my number and I'll confirm it. Their brother is not pesky but is in fact a pretty special guy."

Checking the time and not wanting to miss the ten o'clock curfew Daniel had set, they hurried back to Cayden's apartment with a few minutes to spare. As they pulled into the driveway, Daniel was happy to see no lights on in the garage. When he opened her car door, he mentioned that Don must have trusted him to keep his word and not feel he had to watch for them to come back. Cayden only giggled because she had noticed the upstairs curtains close as Daniel walked around the car.

Allie and Cayden left early Friday morning and talked during the entire two-hour trip to Winchester. That evening, the wedding rehearsal went off without a hitch and the rehearsal dinner was a happy, relaxed time of fellowship and great food. They met Ila and Phillip for breakfast the next morning and spent several hours catching up, with the main conversation centered around Cayden and Daniel's first date. They also touched on the situation Allie faced with Elizabeth and her opposition to the religious education classes.

Phillip quietly worked on his laptop as the girls chatted, interjecting occasionally but otherwise allowing them to enjoy each other's company. When the topic of opposition to the classes came up, he gave them his full attention. He had been impressed that the school system allowed the classes and was sharing how it worked with pastors in other areas, hoping to plant the seed for them to work on having classes in their local schools. Ila was happy when he offered their support if Allie thought it would help. Although she was glad of the offer, Allie explained that a lot of prayer had gone into planning for the meeting and they felt prepared. However, she did ask them to continue praying for the program and also for Elizabeth.

Marta and Wade's wedding was a perfect blend of romance and God's blessing. Before they knew it, the bride and groom were heading to the car to leave for the airport and a lovely honeymoon in Cancun. When Marta turned and tossed the bouquet over her shoulder, it was as if it had a homing device directing it into Cayden's outstretched hands. Turning around, Marta was happy to see her sweet friend's expression turn from shock to a big grin. After hearing all about Cayden and Daniel's first official date, she couldn't help but wonder if maybe they would be hearing wedding bells again in the near future.

Chapter 3

*E*llen Garver, who owned the Shamrock Inn and was one of the sweetest ladies at Southside Baptist, had played a key role in Cayden deciding to apply for the secretary job at Southside and move to Fredericksburg. Earlier in the year, she had taken on a big role in the Feed My Sheep ministry at Southside, where she worked alongside the ministry director, retired Army Chaplain Connor Murphy. She had surprised everyone when Connor was her date for Don and Beth's Memorial Day party, and the couple had been dating ever since.

It, therefore, didn't come as a surprise to Cayden and Beth when they received an invitation for tea at the Shamrock Inn one beautiful Saturday in October. They had been expecting an engagement announcement and hoped this was why Ellen was inviting them over. However, no matter the reason, they would never turn down an opportunity to fellowship with their friend and to enjoy her delicious traditional Irish afternoon tea. Their mouths watered the instant Ellen opened the front door and the aromas, along with her small watchdog Molly, wafted out to greet them.

Not to steal Ellen's thunder, they patiently waited until they were seated at the beautifully appointed table and tea was poured before hinting at the reason for this special treat. When Ellen said nothing and continued chatting about this and that, Beth could stand it no longer. "Okay, are you going to tell us or not?" she blurted out, surprising both her hostess and Cayden.

Seemingly nonplussed by Beth's question, Ellen continued nibbling on an orange scone before wiping her fingers on a cloth napkin and smiling demurely at them. When she spoke, her Irish brogue was a bit more pronounced than usual. "I don't know what you mean, Beth. Can't I just invite my friends over to enjoy their company? You two haven't been here in ages and I thought it was about time." Taking a sip of tea, she continued, "But since you asked, I will admit to an ulterior motive for this special time with you girls. In December, I need you to do me a huge favor, and I thought some baked goodies might sway you to agree to my request." With that, she picked up a small cucumber sandwich and took a dainty bite, while watching Beth's reaction out of the corner of her eye.

Unable to resist the bait Ellen had so sweetly dangled with the mention of a favor, Cayden jumped in before Beth could react, "So what's the favor? We were thinking you were going to tell us you and Connor are engaged, but we're happy to help with a favor."

Now Ellen was beaming at them. "The favor, my sweet girl, is that I need help with wedding plans!" The cat was out of the bag and the three women were hugging and talking all at the same time. When they'd settled back down long enough to talk rationally, Ellen filled them in on this most wonderful announcement. "Connor asked me to marry him just last evening. We have most of the plans nailed down, which was easy because it will be a rather small, intimate wedding. With this being a second marriage for both of us, we want to keep it simple and sweet. His son Shane will be his best man and, Beth, I would love for you to be my matron of honor."

Beth automatically began nodding her head and saying she would love to stand up with her best friend. Ellen went on to say that since she had no children or immediate family in the area, she was going to ask Don to walk her down the aisle.

"Cayden, I'm hoping you'll agree to be my mistress of ceremonies and hostess. You see, we're going to have the wedding and reception here at the inn." Ellen was again watching for reactions from her two friends. She and Connor had made the plans, but she wanted to see how others might perceive them. If Cayden's reaction was any indicator, their plans were going to work out wonderfully.

"Yes, yes, yes!" Cayden almost shouted. "What a great idea! Your house and the gardens will be the perfect backdrop for what I'm sure will be a gorgeous wedding. Are you thinking a large tent in the back yard for the reception? Even if the December weather doesn't cooperate, that will give you lots of extra space for the grand celebration!"

Now, the ladies were in full planning mode. They exchanged ideas, some perfect and some easy to veto, as they sipped Irish tea and enjoyed scrumptious baked treats. By the time Beth and Cayden left for home, Ellen had called Don, who was thrilled to be asked to walk her down the aisle, and the majority of plans were in place.

The months leading up to Thanksgiving, the wedding, and Christmas were busy but also such fun for Cayden and Daniel. They were taking their time getting to know each other. Each phone call, every date, all the laughter, and myriad of shared dreams filled in a picture of who they were and where they envisioned they were heading. Fortunately, it was still too early in their new relationship for any major disagreement. The small misunderstandings or supposed slights they'd experienced thus far were easy to brush aside in the exciting light of new romance. Life was good and it was even better because they were together.

Cayden sometimes attended Daniel's church and was getting to know some of the congregation. While she was faithful at Southside, she occasionally attended Aylett Baptist when they had special weekday services and on a few Sunday evenings. It was exciting to actually see Daniel maturing as he became more at ease and confident in his new role as pastor. This Daniel was a far cry from the man she'd met her first day of work, and she was proud of him.

As autumn was hitting its full stride and leaves were turning lovely colors and falling quietly to earth, the school year was in full swing and Allie was a busy woman. All the usual teacher duties took a lot of time both in the classroom and at home. And always in the back of her mind was the struggle with Elizabeth over the religious education classes. The meeting with Superintendent Barker went well enough, with no disruption of the program or interference with the classes. However, one thing was said that niggled at Allie's mind. Superintendent Barker was very clear that Elizabeth's concerns and observations would not go unheeded. If any other complaints arose, he would consider her input again when he made decisions. Although Elizabeth wasn't happy with the outcome, she seemed mollified enough to let the situation stand for the moment, but Allie kept feeling like she was waiting for the other shoe to drop.

Allie's mom Rae was her biggest cheerleader, and since she often volunteered at the school in various capacities, she had a chance to interact with Elizabeth. In fact, in mid-September she'd been asked to substitute teach in Elizabeth's class while she was out sick. This created a necessity for Elizabeth to talk and email/text with Rae, creating an open dialog between the two women. Elizabeth didn't seem to have a problem with Allie's mom, just Allie.

As Thanksgiving neared, Rae offered her services to teach a special history segment on the first Thanksgiving, and the principal was happy to accept. Rae would work with the third-grade teachers to schedule the appropriate time blocks needed. Strangely enough, Elizabeth seemed to welcome Rae into her classroom and enjoy their time talking. As the holiday drew closer, Rae realized Elizabeth had no plans for spending time with family or even preparing a special meal to enjoy with friends. She had been praying about the situation with Elizabeth for almost three months and was beginning to get to know her a little. What she saw was a woman who apparently had no family in the area and no close friends, a woman who was sad and just didn't know how or what to do to make it better. As she finished her Bible reading one Saturday morning, she decided it was time to talk to her daughter.

When she heard Allie go into the kitchen, she wandered in and took her baby girl in her arms for a long, sweet hug. This was not an unusual thing, but Allie felt that maybe something was on her mother's mind. "You know, Mom, I love your hugs, but I have a feeling this one is to butter me up somehow. Everything okay?"

"Well, since you ask," Rae began, "I do have something I want to discuss with you. I've had this on my heart for the last week or so and can't shake it, but I don't think it will make you happy." As expected, Allie turned her full attention on Rae, tilted her head, and waited. Rae laid out what was on her heart with a big preface. "First, I want you to be sure your happiness and comfort are most important. If you say no to my idea, I'll honor that and leave it alone."

"All of a sudden, I think maybe I'd better sit down. I promise to consider whatever you say and pray about it before answering. How's that?" Allie took her cup of coffee and sat down at the breakfast table, waiting for her mom to continue.

"You know I've found myself working with Elizabeth over the history classes and even subbing for her. You also know I have faithfully been praying for her since the beginning of the school year." Seeing Allie's expression change slightly at the mention of Elizabeth, she decided to just say what she was thinking. "I believe she is so very lonely and doesn't have anywhere or anyone for Thanksgiving, and I'd like to invite her to join our family for our Thanksgiving meal." She'd said all that in one breath and then stood watching her daughter.

Allie just sat there, with no particular expression on her face. Because Rae knew her so well, she could almost see the wheels turning in her brain, but she couldn't determine whether the thoughts were negative or positive. When Allie finally spoke, it was very deliberate, as if the words were being typed out and spoken as she thought them. "I can't say I'm surprised. I knew you were praying and I knew you were spending time with Elizabeth. I was only mildly shocked the other day when you referred to her as 'Liz.' Here's the thing . . . God's been laying it on my heart to invite her to join us too, but I've not been willing to give in. So I asked him just an hour ago to show me definitively what to do." Stopping to wipe tears from her eyes and blow her nose, she finished with, "I guess we'll be setting another plate on the table."

Grabbing her in another bear hug, Rae kissed her daughter's cheek and told her how proud she was of her. Allie smiled at her mom, shook her head, and matter-of-factly said, "But you have to invite her," as she walked out of the kitchen.

Allie was mildly surprised when Elizabeth stopped her in the hall a few days later to thank her for the Thanksgiving invitation. "Your mom was kind to offer, but I wanted to make sure you're okay with me joining your family for dinner."

"Of course, Elizabeth, but you better come hungry. I may be biased, but my mom makes the best Thanksgiving meal and expects to see it eaten." Allie thought that seemed to answer the question, and Elizabeth gave a nod before quickly walking away. Allie wondered yet again how it would all work out.

In addition to Allie's family and Elizabeth, Don and Beth, along with their neighbors Paula and Mrs. Virginia sat around the Lambert's large dining table Thanksgiving afternoon. As Allie had stated, Rae's holiday dinner was excellent. Elizabeth had never seen so much food for one home-cooked meal and was especially awed by the many beautiful dessert dishes filling the kitchen table. Everything about the day had been special and she was glad she'd been brave enough to accept the invitation. However, when board games were brought out for the Lambert Thanksgiving "Game Bowl," she realized it was time for her to leave. For a woman who spent most of her time alone without much social interaction, being part of the large family holiday celebration had been nice, but her senses seemed to be on overload as the jovial smack talk began to ramp up. Rae had seen Elizabeth relax and open up a little as dinner progressed and then begin to close down at the mention of board games. So when Elizabeth thanked her for a lovely meal, Rae didn't try to compel her to stay but instead hugged her before matter-of-factly stating, "Okay, Liz, but you're not leaving here without leftovers. After all, the best part of

Thanksgiving is turkey sandwiches the next day." Relief showed on Elizabeth's face as her hostess filled a bag with several containers, one totally filled with desserts.

Allie walked with Elizabeth to her car and told her how glad they all were that she'd joined them for dinner. Wanting to give her a hug, Allie held back instead, unsure how it would be received. Before she could finish that thought, Elizabeth gave her a quick, rather stiff, hug and said, "Thank you, Allie. It was lovely." As she drove away, a small part of her wanted to put the window down and tell Allie to call her Liz but a larger part that had shut down when her husband died kept her impulse in check. However, she couldn't help but think how nice it would be to feel free and just let her shields down with someone like Allie, who seemed to really want to be her friend.

Cayden and Daniel spent Thanksgiving with his family at his parents' home in Washington, DC. It was Cayden's first time joining them as Daniel's girlfriend and was such fun. Although she really liked all three of his older sisters, she immediately seemed to form a special bond with Julie, probably because she and Daniel were so much alike in both their looks and their personalities. Living in Hampton, Julie knew lots of people in the Virginia Beach area through church activities and homeschooling groups. They were even pleasantly surprised to realize they had several friends in common, which strengthened their connection.

Ila and Phillip were in Texas with friends. Luke and his family had gone skiing in Colorado, while Simon and Coral enjoyed a lively family time with his sister Amy and her family in Fredericksburg. Another Thanksgiving came to a close with happy memories of blessings beyond measure, including friends, family, great food, and—most importantly—a loving Savior whose birthday would be celebrated in a few weeks.

After Thanksgiving, time seemed to fly. While everyone else was busy with Christmas plans, shopping, and decorating, Ellen and Connor were finishing up last-minute projects in order to be ready for their wedding. Ellen and Faye, a friend from Dublin who had always wanted to visit the United States, were swapping houses for two months. Faye would help at the inn and have some time for sightseeing while Ellen and Connor enjoyed leisurely touring Ireland.

Cayden was happily keeping tabs on many of the wedding preparations with her trusty spreadsheets. Invitations had been hand delivered. The tent would be erected two days before the ceremony and the caterer would take care of all setup, food, and cleanup. Music was lined up to play quietly before the ceremony and less quietly during the reception, with a harpist to play during the ceremony itself. Everything was coming together and Ellen's wedding would be as lovely as the bride herself. Two weeks and counting!

When Allie arrived at school the Monday after Thanksgiving, she wasn't sure what to expect from Elizabeth. While their tentative relationship seemed a bit friendlier, the religious education issue between them was not resolved. As she was putting her coat and purse away and preparing for her small wards, Elizabeth popped her head in the door, said good morning, thanked her again for Thanksgiving, and popped back out. Allie relaxed and thanked her Lord for working in their lives. She'd have to remember to thank her family and friends for praying.

Ila and Phillip arrived back in Fredericksburg the week after Thanksgiving and would stay in the general vicinity for the holidays. Happy to have everyone home, Allie insisted they meet at Olaf's for dinner one evening and all agreed it was time to catch up. Their group was a bit larger than it had been just a year earlier. In addition to the original six (Allie, Ila, Cayden, Luke, Phillip, Daniel), they now welcomed Simon and Coral, along with Allie's brothers. Gil and Joey had recently begun attending Daniel's church and when they arrived at Olaf's, they also brought Brandon Printz, Cayden's high school friend who lived in Glen Allen and also attended Aylett Baptist. Olaf greeted them with hugs and slaps on the back before instructing his waitstaff to treat his brothers and sisters with outstanding service.

The group was also different because this year there were two married couples and one dating couple. Also, many of their circumstances had changed over time as life does and they all agreed God's hand was evident in their lives. Cayden found herself noticing a change in Allie and Luke's relationship too. Luke's long-time girlfriend had recently accepted a new job in Kansas and they had parted as friends. Allie had been in a semi-serious relationship at the first of the year, but that had ended amicably also. Anytime they went out as a group, the two paired off without even realizing it and Cayden often caught Luke watching Allie. Smiling to herself, she thought seeing how this might work out was going to be interesting because both Luke and Allie could be a bit oblivious when it came to someone paying them attention and they had grown up together, which added to the possibility they might overlook the fact they were pretty much perfect for each other.

The day before Ellen and Connor's wedding, snow fell off and on, leaving two inches of fluffy white snow on the ground and trees. It had begun just after the tables and chairs were set up in the tent and all was ready for the reception. Not to be deterred by something so beautiful, Ellen reveled in how lovely the back yard looked. If the weatherman was right, another inch might fall overnight, but then the sun would shine on her wedding day. Although she hadn't thought another man could fill her heart with such love after her Niall passed, she was happily looking forward to spending the rest of her days with Connor, a man she loved with all her heart. God was so good!

As predicted, the sun was hesitantly shining the next day as Ellen and Connor pledged their love to each other and Pastor Harwell pronounced them husband and wife. They were such a striking couple—he in his Army dress blue uniform and she in a vintage pale blue linen Chanel suit and a pillbox hat with veil. Although the short service was very calm and stately, the reception was a bit livelier as those gathered enjoyed a delicious meal comprised of Irish dishes some had never tasted but thoroughly enjoyed. Along with the beautiful wedding cake, there were also goodie boxes filled with small pastries and cakes Ellen had made for each guest to take home as a thank you for making their wedding so special. Shortly after everyone finished lunch, the couple was on their way to the airport. God had blessed Ellen and Connor with love a second time and they were excited to face each new adventure together. Tomorrow they would be in the Emerald Isle and they would spend this Christmas in Killarney.

Chapter 4

Christmas passed in a blur for Cayden. She and Daniel spent Christmas Eve and Christmas with her family in Virginia and planned to be at his folks' for a big New Year's Eve party. They celebrated Daniel's Christmas Eve birthday with a wonderful family dinner topped off with her mom's famous cheesecake. His gift from her mom was the promise of a whole cheesecake with his name on it in the refrigerator for him to take back home. Daniel was a happy man—celebrating Christmas with Cayden and cheesecake—he couldn't ask for more.

Upon returning home, Cayden called Allie and Ila and invited them over the next evening for girls' night. With Ila out of town a lot of the time, they hadn't had much time to just sit around, snack, and chat in what seemed like forever.

Allie arrived first carrying a large platter of goodies, with Ila close on her heels bringing their order from Chick-fil-A and a new game she'd gotten for Christmas. As hostess, Cayden provided the sweet tea, coffee, hot cocoa, and her mom's cheesecake. A prayer of thanks for their food and friendship and they were off to the races. It was time to hear all about what had happened over Christmas.

Ila kicked it off with, "Okay, last year I started things off because it was my first Christmas with Phillip. So unless Allie disagrees, Cayden, my girl, you're up first." Seeing Allie nod her agreement, she continued, "How was your first Christmas as a couple?"

Cayden began with a long, drawn-out, "Well…" and then jumped into how wonderful it had been. "It was so much fun buying gifts for Daniel and then seeing his excitement opening them. Sorry if that sounds like I'm referring to a toddler, but you know what I mean. All these 'firsts' are so cool!"

"And how was it with your family?" Allie prompted. "That was Daniel's first trip to Virginia Beach with you, right? Did he fit in or are you banned from ever bringing him again?" She finished that off with a chuckle because pretty much everyone young and old liked Daniel. That was one thing that made him a great pastor.

"Oh, he fit in all right. You know that pesky brother concern I had when I first met him? Well, it showed itself briefly a few times when he and Carter would gang up on me when we played games. Of course, that was their tactic to distract the reigning champion so I had to forgive him, and he always apologized in the sweetest way so that I couldn't actually get angry. I could, however, get even and that was fun too!" Even she could hear the sappy tone of her voice, which meant it was time to move on. "So, Allie, how was your Christmas on the farm?"

"Not much to report. In fact, it was borderline boring. The boys invited Brandon over one night for dinner and we played some new Nintendo games. Otherwise, it was quiet but I have to admit it was okay in the long run because the school year has been so stressful thanks to Elizabeth's objections to our religious education classes." Shaking her head and looking sort of conflicted, Allie confessed her confusion where Elizabeth was concerned. "It's not unlike riding a roller coaster—you know, one of those that has corkscrew turns and huge drops. I just can't understand her and sometimes want to give up, but then I can't because I'm sure there's something bothering her and she needs help. You don't know how grateful I am to know you all are praying."

Nodding along with Cayden, Ila chimed in, "We're all praying and I'm so glad you're not giving up on her. God's got this, but remember that with Him it's not about time but timing." Realizing it was now her turn, she continued. "Our Christmas was wonderful from start to finish and mainly because we were celebrating Jesus together as husband and wife this year. Both sets of parents came up for Christmas Day, and we had a great meal and enjoyed just sitting around visiting until early evening. Since our apartment is too small for company to spend the night, they stayed at the Shamrock Inn, where we joined them for breakfast the next morning. Even with Ellen on her honeymoon, the pastries are still to die for. Faye asked about you girls and sends her love."

Talk continued with updates on the Feed My Sheep ministry, family, and friends until Ila realized the time and announced that she'd promised to be home before too late. Allie agreed she needed to get on home too, since she was going skiing with her brothers and Luke the next morning. At her casual mention of Luke, Ila's eyebrows went up a tad as she looked over at Cayden, who only nodded, which meant they would talk later. Allie and Luke, huh? Well, well, well, no telling what the new year would bring to their little trio.

Christmas break was a hard time for Elizabeth. She had traveled to her parents' home in Pennsylvania on Christmas Eve and returned home the day after Christmas, which left a large part of the two-week break with not a lot to do. Her orange tabby cat, Perseus, was glad to have her back home. He had been a good excuse to stay only two days with her parents. The holidays just didn't mean a lot to her anymore, and she recognized she didn't add a lot to the festivities her mother and father enjoyed. They were better off without her there to put a damper on things.

When she and Chris first married, they were the life of any party. After he was assigned to Fort A.P. Hill not far from Fredericksburg, they made it a point to try and get back home to celebrate Christmas with their families. Life held so much promise then—the hope of children, growing old with each other, travel, all the normal expectations of a young couple. But that came to an abrupt end when Chris took his motorcycle out for a drive in the countryside one Saturday afternoon so that she could have some peace and quiet in order to catch up on things around the house. He never came back home. The police officers who arrived at her door just as she was beginning to work on dinner were kind. The woman officer tried to console her as her world shattered around her, but no one could help. A young Army chaplain came later that night and Elizabeth held it together long enough to assure him she would be fine. He seemed glad to escape.

After the funeral, she had decided to stay in Virginia. Their house in the Lake Caroline community was her home and she couldn't even think of leaving it to return to Pennsylvania. While Chris's life insurance was enough to almost pay off the mortgage, Elizabeth soon realized she would need to find a job. With her education and teaching experience, it was easy to obtain her Virginia teaching certification, and it didn't take long to land the job in Ladysmith. That had been her salvation. It gave her purpose and she loved the children. She had her house, her cat, and her job.

She had been raised in a family that went to church for special occasions and holidays but had no desire to delve deeper into "all that stuff," as her father would say. Her grandmother was the only person to ever actually talk to her about Jesus when she visited her grandmother's farm as a child. She and Chris had decided to do better when they moved to Virginia and had joined a church, attending most Sunday mornings. They felt comfortable that their belief in God's existence was sufficient for their spiritual well-being. When Chris died, their pastor had performed a memorial service, and his ashes had been spread on her grandmother's farm in Pennsylvania. Now, with Chris gone and her life so meaningless, Elizabeth took no time to even think about God, and when He did come to mind it was with a simmering anger at what He had allowed to happen.

Rae had invited her to a New Year's Eve party at their farm, but Elizabeth preferred to sleep through the heralding of a new year. After all, what would be different after midnight other than the need to remember to write or type the correct year, 2019, on a check or document? Nothing.

At work, Allie noticed that Elizabeth seemed to have drawn back into the sullen woman she had been at the beginning of the school year. When she mentioned it to her mom, Rae agreed it was noticeable and they began to pray, interceding for this woman God kept putting on their hearts to care about and try to love through Him.

Returning to school in the new year was always interesting for Allie. The children almost had to be reoriented with their daily classroom routine, and many of them longed for the days of sleeping late and playing all day. Some of the teachers fell into the same category, but soon the regular school day was in full swing as if a two-week break hadn't even happened. Allie's day went pretty much as usual until after lunch, when two of her students complained of tummy aches. Her aide was able to accompany one little boy to the nurse with no mishap. However, Allie wasn't so lucky. Betsy, a sweet natured, quiet girl, made it only into the hallway before her lunch came back up all over Allie's skirt and shoes. Glad for her mom's advice to keep spare clothes in her locker and another set in her car, Allie was able to make herself presentable enough to finish the one hour before the bell rang to end the day. She was looking forward to getting home, taking a shower, and probably throwing her shoes in the trash. As she pulled in the driveway, she saw Luke standing on the back porch with Gil and Joey, which effectively gave her no choice but to walk by them in order to enter the house. As she opened the car door, the fresh air was heavenly and she realized was a good indicator of how she must reek. Deciding to make the best of it, she quickly warned the guys, "You may want to move away from the door. Betsy had a tummy problem this afternoon and I need to freshen up before anyone comes near me. So consider yourselves warned." And, with that, she dashed for the door and straight upstairs, leaving only a slight odor trail behind her.

When she came downstairs later, Luke and her brothers were in the den. Rae was working on dinner and her dad was "helping" by sipping coffee, chatting with her mom, and staying out of her way.

"There you are. The boys told us what happened. They even pulled your car into the garage in order to leave the windows open and air it out. Your clothes are in the wash and your shoes, sadly enough, are history." Giving Allie a hug, Rae reminded her, "Such is the life of a third-grade teacher!"

Her dad chimed in with, "I made them promise not to tease you over dinner but you know your brothers. Luke's staying for dinner and, as a teacher, I'm sure he totally understands."

At the mention of Luke, Allie stopped and for the first time realized he'd been a witness to the mess she had been earlier. Surprised that it mattered to her since, as her dad said, Luke would surely sympathize with her, she shrugged it off and helped Rae finish getting dinner on the table. When her brothers started to rib her about halfway through the meal, Luke rerouted the conversation to their skiing trip after Christmas and her brothers were sidetracked into planning a return visit. Allie silently mouthed "thank you" to Luke, who only smiled before they both joined the planning discussion. Skiing had been such fun pairing off with one of her brothers or Luke, and she was more than game to go again.

Luke also thought skiing with the Lamberts had been fun, but he especially enjoyed the times he paired off with Allie. She was a really good skier and could hold her own with any of them. It didn't hurt that she was also a lot of fun to be around and easy to talk with. They had known each other forever, but he was just now beginning to see the grown-up Allie Lambert and she was quite interesting.

Daniel's congregation was seeing significant growth since the new year began. Faith Haverly, who had recently moved to Aylett from Newport News, joined the church in early January. Her Aunt Georgia, a long-time member and recent widow, was more than happy to have Faith living with her. Her talents included singing and playing piano, and she was a great addition to the single adults group according to Gil, Joey, and Brandon.

Cayden and Allie were happy when they were included in any of the single adults group activities, and the addition of another twenty-something woman who could really bowl was just what they needed. The guys all took bowling seriously, and Faith helped level the playing field when the teams were guys versus gals.

The new year also brought sadness to their ranks when Coral miscarried and she and Simon received news from her doctors that she would in all likelihood never be physically able to carry a baby. With Coral and Simon being relatively new to Southside and their small group of friends, none of them knew a problem existed until the miscarriage, which had been one of several over the last couple of years. Soon, a support network was in place surrounding Simon and Coral with love, encouragement, and prayer. Beth and Don, who had experienced a somewhat similar situation in their younger days, were front and center lending a listening ear, a helping hand, and a shoulder to lean on.

Through prayer and support from family and friends, Coral and Simon decided to pursue adoption. It wasn't long before they were feeling hopeful for adoption of a baby from an orphanage in China. They were working through a faith-based organization, and the wheels were in motion. Hopes were that by mid-2020 they would realize success and bring home a child to love and raise as their own.

In the meantime, they also started the process of becoming approved as foster parents, something they had contemplated previously just in case they were needed to help in emergency situations. With Simon's line of work, they had seen many situations where they wished they could help but couldn't because they were not approved by the state to care for children in their home. Taking this step made both of them feel they were at least doing something useful to possibly help nurture a child or children at a time when it was needed most.

Chapter 5

Near the end of January, Rae had the chance to spend some time with Elizabeth working on a play the students would perform for Presidents' Day the following month. Something was mentioned about the religious education class, and Elizabeth seemed to just boil over with something akin to hatred. She began to rant even more than she'd done on previous occasions, and Rae found herself asking the Father for guidance on how to proceed.

"Liz, I've got to stop you before you say something you'll regret. Or maybe it will be something I regret, because I have come to think of you as a special friend. But I will not stand here and listen to you disrespect the Lord. I also won't allow you to malign my daughter and the other teachers just because you're not happy." Taking a second to see how what she was saying was being received, she was surprised to see Elizabeth almost deflate in front of her. The bristling, angry woman from a minute earlier now looked like all the fight had gone out of her and she was about to keel over. Helping her to a seat, Rae took her hands and did the only thing she could think to do—pray. "Dear Father, please help us. Only you know what's going on in Elizabeth's heart and mind, which means only you can help her. Help me to be what she needs, Lord. Thank you. Amen."

Still silent, Elizabeth sat straighter but seemed shaken by the intensity of her emotions. Rae also sat quietly, listening to what the Holy Spirit was prompting her to do next.

"Okay, sweet girl, I've not pressed you about anything regarding religion or spiritual matters, and I won't now. But I have to tell you that you need help and that help is Jesus." Rae stopped as she saw Elizabeth shifting in her chair as if getting ready to speak. "I believe your strong emotions concerning the religious education class are coming from something deeper seated in you, but I have to say that your reaction just now is out of proportion to the situation." Again, Elizabeth seemed ready to speak, but Rae lifted her hand before she could say anything and simply asked one question. "Have you even attended one of the classes to see what you're railing against?"

This seemed to make Elizabeth stop and think. "No, I haven't. My argument is a blanket argument against any type of religious teaching in the school. But to be fair to the majority who obviously see value in it, I suppose that makes logical sense." Rae's face must have reflected the shock she was feeling at Elizabeth's statement because Elizabeth suddenly started laughing, something Rae had only heard a couple of times before. "Sorry, Rae, about my outburst and thank you for being a good friend to intervene. I'll make it a point to attend the next class."

After that, they finished their planned work and parted ways. Rae was a bit shaken at the turn of events, but then the Holy Spirit impressed on her these questions, "Rae, why are you shaken and surprised? Isn't this what you've been praying for?" On the way to her car, Rae cried, praised, and thanked the Lord.

Even knowing that Elizabeth planned to attend one of the religious education classes, it still threw Allie when she came in and sat at the back of the room. Elizabeth was such an unknown—surly one minute, ambivalent another—that it was hard to relax around her. So with prayer in her heart and thanksgiving on her tongue, Allie started the class with prayer and launched into the lesson God had laid on her heart just last night. It was one of the simplest lessons for smaller children, especially, to grasp and it was always a plus when there was a catchy song with fun hand motions to help get the point across.

As Elizabeth listened intently, first to see what fault she might find and then because the lesson was sort of familiar, she remembered her grandmother teaching her a song about a wee little man named Zacchaeus who climbed a sycamore tree so that he could see who Jesus was. Elizabeth had loved to climb trees back then, so the song intrigued her. Her grandmother had talked about how wonderful it was that Jesus hadn't met Zacchaeus before but He called him by name and said, "I'm going to your house today." Grandmother had said it was important for everyone, no matter how little, to ask Jesus to come live in their heart. Although she hadn't understood what that meant, it stuck in her mind that if her grandmother said it was important, then it really must be. As she picked back up with Allie's telling of the story, she heard one thing and that was, "For the Son of man is come to seek and to save that which was lost." She didn't understand that, either, but it made her almost gasp. Not understanding her reaction to a phrase she couldn't even begin to explain, she quickly stood up and left the room as the children were singing happily about Zacchaeus.

Allie saw Elizabeth almost flee from the room and wondered if something was physically wrong with her or if she had just heard enough to make her even more determined to stop the classes. She motioned to Jeanine to take over the class and then went in search of Elizabeth. When she couldn't find her, she checked at the front office and learned that Elizabeth had gone home sick. Still not sure what was happening, Allie phoned her mom to ask her to pray. Then she texted Cayden asking her to send a text to the church prayer chain group asking for them to pray for an unspoken need.

Rae couldn't get Elizabeth off her mind the rest of the morning. What if the girl was at home alone and ill? Or what if she was having another meltdown similar to earlier in the week? That wasn't really healthy, either. After trying to call her a couple of times with the calls going straight to voicemail, Rae decided action was in order. She stopped long enough to grab her Bible and a container of chicken vegetable soup from the freezer before setting out to learn just what was what. The short trip to Lake Caroline was made in record time with lots of communication between Rae and Jesus, which resulted in a calm spirit and a heart ready to console and offer assistance, whatever might be needed. In her heart she knew Elizabeth was in trouble and she had to help.

She pulled into the driveway of a neat weathered gray chalet with a barn red front door and shutters. At first, there was no answer to Rae's pressing the doorbell button, but she knew Elizabeth was home because her car was in the driveway. Not one to give up easily, she rang it several more times before venturing around to the back, where she spotted Elizabeth sitting on the deck with her head in her hands, weeping. As Elizabeth heard Rae call out a greeting, she jumped to her feet and met her halfway across the back yard.

"What are you doing here?" was all she could manage to say between sobs. Instead of answering, Rae folded her into a motherly hug that seemed to open a floodgate of tears in the younger woman. As Elizabeth allowed herself to be comforted, she realized she had no real idea why she was crying, but she knew it had been a long time coming and she had no way to stop. Rae crooned as she held on tightly, just like she'd always done with her children, a natural mother's reaction to help a child in distress. Eventually, the sobs subsided and the tears lessened.

"I'm here because my newest friend needs help and I desperately want to help her if I can." Backing up and looking Elizabeth in the eyes she could see clarity and a bit of calm returning, or at least less stress in her face. "I even brought chicken soup in case you were ill." This brought a small smile, which was Rae's intent, and they both sat down on the deck settee.

"Put your mind at ease. I'm not ill. To be honest with you, I don't know what I am. Tears are usually not my thing." Stopping to wipe away tears and get more tissues, she went one step further. "I haven't really cried in four years since my husband died."

Taken aback and not totally sure how to react, Rae went where she felt the Holy Spirit was leading. "I am so sorry, Liz. I wasn't aware you'd ever been married let alone lost your husband."

"When I interviewed for my job, I was adamant that details of my private life be kept confidential. Now, I'm not so sure that was the wisest choice. You know what they say: Hindsight is twenty-twenty." After taking a minute to regroup, she continued. "Allie's lesson today brought back memories from my childhood when I'd visit my grandmother during the summer. She told me about Zacchaeus and that I needed to ask Jesus into my heart, which made no sense then and makes none now. Allie's lesson combined with my grandmother's words overwhelmed me and I had to get out of that room. At least I had the presence of mind to stop by the office and let them know I was leaving." She looked at her only friend in the world as tears started again, and she simply stated, "Rae, I'm so very tired."

Seeing the girl was exhausted, Rae helped her into the house and made sure she had everything she needed, including her and Allie's numbers. "Just one thing and I'll leave you to get some rest. I understand you've met your neighbor, Daniel Garrett. His house is located on a lot on Ladysmith Lake. He said you've talked at HOA meetings. I'm going to also jot his number down since he lives closer and can be here quicker than we can. He is a pastor and a really good man, and I know he would love to assist you in any way he can." After putting the soup in the refrigerator, Rae let herself out and sat in her car for a few minutes, pouring her heart out to the Father as she felt the Holy Spirit soothing her heart and soul. Unbeknownst to her, He was also spreading peace and comfort to the young lady who had just begun to reach out to Him, even though she didn't know it yet.

Knowing that Elizabeth wanted to keep her personal life confidential, Rae couldn't in all good conscience share their conversation with Allie. When Allie got home from school, Rae told her only that Elizabeth wasn't ill and that her abrupt departure from the classroom had nothing to do with the school's religious education classes. Being an observant, caring woman, Allie deduced there was more to the situation than her mom shared and that her mom was definitely concerned about her new friend. Noticing dinner prep hadn't yet begun, Allie announced she was ordering pizza and wings and a large salad. She and Rae were both happy to settle in for the evening without another chore to complete. After all, any cleanup could be taken care of by the male contingent of their family.

Chapter 6

*F*ebruary was a cold, dreary month with temperatures constantly below freezing and a couple of small snow showers but nothing significant. On the second Sunday of the month, everyone was happy to welcome Ellen and Connor back home after their two-month honeymoon. After church that night, a large group followed them back to the Shamrock Inn to enjoy refreshments and lots of tales from their adventures in Ireland.

In her heaviest Irish brogue, Ellen reported, "It was wonderful craic even if we did grow a wee bit homesick for the states. And though Connor wasn't too fond of a hearty fry-up, he did enjoy lunch or supper at the local chipper." Clearing her voice and dropping the heavy accent, she added, "All that to say that we had a wonderfully fun time and Connor definitely preferred fish and chips over a traditional full breakfast."

When asked if he liked the full Irish breakfast, Connor wasn't shy to say, "Even though my family roots are in Ireland, my stomach, especially in the mornings, is totally American. Rashers are great but I never again wish to try black and white pudding!"

"One morning, we decided to go out to eat and all the poor man wanted was a fried egg, bacon, and a piece of toast. He explained that he wanted the egg cooked hard, but it arrived in a full Irish breakfast with a runny yolk. So he tried again using his hands to describe how the cook should firmly press down on the egg so that the yolk was fully cooked."

As everyone chuckled, Connor picked up the story, "As Ellen enjoyed her breakfast that had been cooked perfectly to her directions, I waited patiently. After all, we didn't have anywhere else to be and I was now determined that our very Irish waiter see what a correctly cooked fried egg looks like."

When Connor stopped to sip his coffee, Don spoke up, "Don't keep us in suspense. Did they get it right?" which, of course, had everyone laughing.

"Nope! He came back to the table with an egg that had been cooked a little longer but still not long enough to fully cook the yolk, and they'd added more black and white pudding as a way to apologize for any inconvenience." At this point, he nodded and waved his hand at his wife, who was dying to tell what happened next.

"My very kind, patient, Irish-American husband looked at the waiter and asked if he could possibly go into the kitchen and show the cook how to cook an egg properly!" By this time, she was laughing so hard she could hardly speak, and the rest of the group was joining in with her. "Before the waiter could reply, Connor got up and walked into the kitchen. A few minutes later, he walked back out with two eggs cooked to his specifications and to a room full of applause! And, there was no black and white pudding on his plate!"

On that hilarious note, people began gathering their coats and thanking their host and hostess. It was a bright spot in their cold winter to have two of their favorite people back home safe and sound, and they knew many more stories of their adventures would be shared over the next month or so as Ellen and Connor settled into married life at the inn.

With Valentine's Day quickly approaching, Daniel began thinking about how best to make it extra special for Cayden. When his sister Julie called to check up on her baby brother, he decided to ask for her advice. After all, she and Jimmy had been married for over ten years and always seemed quite happy. She listened patiently as he shared several grandiose ideas he'd been considering before asking a very simple question. "Daniel, do any of those plans sound like Cayden?" Hearing only a sigh from her brother, she continued, "It's a week night, which means not a lot of time to get home and changed or to travel into Richmond. Maybe plan a simple yet elegant evening with a wonderful dinner, some chocolates, and a lovely gift." Coming to a full stop, she added, "Wait a minute! What kind of gift are you considering? A ring?"

Daniel's laughter answered the last question. No, there wouldn't be a ring just yet. But Julie's common sense advice did work to get him thinking of a brand new plan.

The following morning a single red rose was delivered to Cayden at work with a handwritten invitation for Miss Cayden Dewitt to join Mr. Daniel

Garrett at his home at six-thirty the night of February 14 for a four-course meal and a movie of her choosing. She was requested to RSVP via text to Daniel's phone, which she promptly took care of by texting this message: *Miss Cayden Dewitt is delighted to accept Mr. Garrett's kind and oh so sweet invitation.* A return text acknowledged her acceptance and advised a car and driver would be at her residence at six that evening and that Mr. Garrett would be most happy to take her home afterward. Cayden was almost too giddy to work after Daniel's romantic gestures, and she decided to call Allie. It was time to shop for a new outfit.

No amount of questioning or cajoling could get Daniel to divulge more information about their Valentine's Day evening, which added to the fun and excitement. When someone knocked on her door promptly at six, she was surprised to see one of the young men from Southside in a black suit, white shirt, red tie, and black hat ready to escort her downstairs. As she settled into the back seat of a black SUV that belonged to the young man's father, he handed her a single pink rose with a note attached, which simply said "Thinking of you." The half-hour drive seemed to fly as she thought of Daniel and their journey to this point and where they were headed next.

To say the night was a huge success would be an understatement. They took their time with each course of the meal Daniel had spent the afternoon preparing, deciding to save the decadent chocolate cake with chocolate ganache and frosting for after the movie. Cayden was absolutely blown away by his cooking and planning skills, not to mention just how sweet everything he'd done was. Daniel was prepared with a list of movies that Cayden might like (thanks to Julie), and the list was a big hit. Her final choice was titled *Fireproof,* a story of love and relationship restoration with a happy ending.

As the ending movie credits rolled, Daniel served coffee and cake, along with a large beautifully wrapped box. Halfway through dessert, he couldn't wait any longer and told her to open her gift. Not even trying to hide her excitement, she sat on the floor and quickly started ripping the paper off. Laughing, she jumped up and hugged him before sitting back down to examine her gift more closely. For Christmas, her grandmother had given her several albums from her extensive collection of vintage records, but she had nothing on which to play them. How thoughtful that Daniel had remembered and had given her a record player. Just as she was about to get up and give him his gift, she noticed a smaller rectangular shaped gift in the bottom of the large box. Looking up at Daniel, she smiled and asked innocently, "Is that mine too?" When he nodded, she gently opened the gift, savoring each movement. This box looked quite interesting. She caught her breath when she saw the delicate gold chain and heart pendant surrounded with tiny diamonds. "Oh, Daniel, this is exquisite," she whispered through tears.

Taking her by the hands, he helped her up and gave her a hug before taking the necklace and placing it around her neck. "I hope you already know you have my heart. This is just a reminder." Realizing this was the first time he'd spoken so directly to her about his feelings, he led her to the sofa and they sat down, quiet for just a minute, before he spoke again.

"Cayden, I do love you and I find myself happily looking forward to each day to see what happens next in our relationship." Seeing more tears rolling down her cheeks, he continued. "I hope you don't mind it wasn't a ring."

"Oh, Daniel, I love you too, but I'm glad it wasn't a ring. I'm enjoying taking our time really getting to know each other, and this dating phase of our relationship is fun. We've both had a lot of 'firsts' with necessary adjustments to our lives recently, so I vote to keep on the path we're on until God shows us it's time for the next step." She fingered the heart pendant and waited to hear how he would respond.

"It's funny how we think so much alike most of the time, and I'm glad we're in agreement to just enjoy what He has for us and follow where He leads. My heart tells me it will one day lead to marriage because I can't imagine loving anyone more than I love you." Another quick hug and he led her out the door to take her home. As he turned to lock the door, he spied a wrapped package leaning against the wall.

Cayden gasped and started laughing. "I got so excited with my gifts, I totally forgot about yours. I wanted it to be a surprise so I left it out here in case the odd-shaped packaging might be a tip off to what's inside." Laughing, they went back inside where he unwrapped a fishing rod and reel. "I heard you telling your dad about a particular rod you were planning to buy. So I called him and he was more than happy to tell me exactly what to get and where to get it. And, by the way, Tad at Bass Pro Shops said to tell you hello." She had been a bit taken aback when the young man at the store commented on her unusual name and then asked if she knew Pastor Garrett. Further conversation revealed that Daniel was Tad's pastor and that he had heard Cayden's name mentioned more than once, something that thrilled her heart to hear.

Daniel stopped examining his new toy long enough to properly thank Cayden and give her a hug. If he'd had any doubts, he now knew for sure and certain this woman was a keeper!

The day after Valentine's Day was a big day for the third graders and Elizabeth. With Rae's help, she felt the children were ready to present their play titled *Our Founding Fathers*. After her meltdown a couple of weeks earlier, her mind seemed clearer even though nothing had really changed. Maybe tears had cleansing powers or maybe she had just needed to clear out some of the cobwebs that had built up in her mind over the years. Regardless, the big day was here and she was determined to enjoy every moment of the kids' excitement. It was a huge success according to all the teachers and parents.

As Elizabeth walked to her car after school was dismissed, Allie caught up with her to offer congratulations and thanks for all the hard work she'd poured into the play. As an afterthought, she added, "I've been hankering for some good barbecue and am planning to go into Ashland for dinner. Would you want to join me? I could stop by and pick you up around six and the company would be appreciated." Seeing Elizabeth's hesitation, she added, "Maybe we could discuss another play for the children before the end of the school year." That seemed to turn the tide and Elizabeth agreed to dinner but said she would meet Allie at the restaurant. Not wanting to read too much into this small step forward, Allie just smiled, but inside she was praising the Lord.

After they placed their orders, their conversation started off a little stilted but quickly became more comfortable as they talked about the play and their students. Elizabeth surprised Allie when she apologized for abruptly leaving the religious education class. "I guess your mom filled you in on what triggered my actions," she ended with a sigh.

"No, Mom only told me you were not ill and that your departure had nothing to do with the class, both of which put my mind at ease. I didn't think it my place to pry even though I'd like to know if there's anything I can do to help in some way." Allie's assurance came just as the waiter delivered their food and conversation turned to more general topics.

As they were finishing their barbecue, Elizabeth began sharing some of the things she'd discussed with Rae. Allie was surprised to learn Elizabeth was a widow, and her heart began to ache for this young woman who had faced so much alone.

"When Chris died, part of me died too. I've become quite adept at closing myself off from others and usually have no problem with it. However, lately I've found myself feeling lonely and wishing I had more in my life than work and my cat." Giving a short laugh at how that sounded, she continued, "I blame you and your family for this turn of events."

It was Allie's turn to laugh now and ask how her family could possibly be responsible for the change in her thinking. "But I must say that I'm glad if we are playing a part in you wanting to open your life up to interaction with others. Also, I'll say that I hope you will let us be a part of your life going forward." In an attempt to lighten the mood, she added, "Of course, we can leave Gil and Joey out of the equation if that's a deal breaker. I know just how annoying they can be."

As they paid their tabs and were getting in their cars, both women felt lighter and happier. Elizabeth even went so far as to ask Allie to call her Liz, which Allie saw as a huge stride in their relationship. Since it was still early, she invited Liz to come by the house for dessert. "Mom has a coconut cream pie in the refrigerator. Well, she actually has two because one would never suffice with my dad and brothers around. We can settle in with mom for a little girl talk. She would love it and so would I. What do you say?" Surprisingly, Liz agreed, and Allie gave her mom a call to let her know to save some pie for them.

The ladies enjoyed coffee and pie in the den while chatting comfortably. Rae was quick to pick up on Allie referring to their guest as Liz and that made her heart happy. Although she already knew it to be true, she rejoiced to see outward signs that God was working in their friend's heart. She was happy when Liz brought up the lesson Allie had been teaching about Zacchaeus during the religious education class.

"My grandmother taught me about Zacchaeus and said everyone needed to ask Jesus into their heart. That's been playing in my mind ever since and I'd like to understand." Turning to Rae, she continued, "That day, when I said I was tired, you so kindly ministered to my physical needs. But even though I was physically exhausted from crying, I've also become so very tired of being lonely, living in a miserable bubble of my own making. Can you help me understand?"

Sensing this was a conversation between Liz and Rae, Allie excused herself to make more coffee. In the kitchen, she started a new pot of coffee but her main objective was to pray. Liz was opening up, and Allie prayed with all her heart that her friend, this woman who had been an antagonist for months, would accept the gift of salvation Jesus offered.

Settling back in her chair, Rae spoke with tenderness and confidence. "Your grandmother knew what Zacchaeus was just beginning to understand. He had to have heard of the miracles Jesus performed—feeding multitudes of people from a boy's lunch; healing the deaf, blind, and lame; and even raising Lazarus from the dead. He must also have heard that Jesus was the promised Messiah and he was curious. So much so that he did whatever he needed to do to see Jesus as He passed through his hometown, climb a tree." She stopped to sip her coffee but to also gauge how Liz was accepting what she was sharing with her. When she saw only a look of someone waiting for what would come next, she continued with a very important question, "Liz, do you believe God exists?"

With tears in her eyes and without a second's hesitation, Liz replied, "Yes, I know God exists because I've been angry at Him since Chris died, and it's not possible to be this angry at someone who doesn't exist. We were so young and had our whole lives ahead of us. We were supposed to have children, travel, and grow old together. Then, he was gone. He left home for a stupid motorcycle ride and never came back to me. For years, I've curled up into this tight ball of anger and I'm tired of it. Tired of feeling so alone, tired of the fury that sometimes threatens to destroy me. I just don't know how to let it go, how to stop being angry."

Moving her chair closer to Liz, Rae took her hands before asking, "Are you ready to stop blaming God and let Him into your life? He loves you so much and He's patiently waiting for you to see that you need Him. Zacchaeus had come to the point where he recognized he needed what Jesus was offering—forgiveness of sins, peace, and rest for his soul. That's why he sought Jesus out that day, just like you're doing right now."

"But God can't want to have anything to do with me. If He really is all-knowing, then He knows the furious, wicked person I am and I don't deserve anything from Him." Tears were freely flowing down her cheeks as she considered the condition of her heart and why God couldn't possibly want any part of her.

Rae got up to retrieve the tissue box before she continued. "Zacchaeus was a Jew who collected taxes for the Romans and everyone despised him, but it was his house that Jesus chose to visit that day. It was Zacchaeus that Jesus called by name, just like I believe He's calling you by your name right now. He's known you since before you were born and loves you no matter what. Would you like to answer His call? He's been waiting a long time for you because He loves you so much, but He would never force you to love Him back. It's a choice we all have to make, just like your grandmother said."

Looking at Liz was like looking at the sun beginning to peek through the clouds as she was starting to accept that all Rae was saying was true. With a tentative smile and tears still streaming, Liz asked, "Can you help me? I don't know what to do."

Taking her Bible, Rae read several verses and made sure Liz understood their meaning before going on to the next. "For all have sinned, and come short of the glory of God" (Romans 3:23 KJV). "For the wages of sin is death" (Romans 6:23 KJV). "But God commendeth his love toward us, in that, while we were yet sinners, Christ died for us" (Romans 5:8 KJV). "For whosoever shall call upon the name of the Lord shall be saved" (Romans 10:13 KJV).

"Liz, all you have to do is believe and ask Jesus to forgive you of your sins. He wants you to love Him and have a close relationship with Him. Are you ready to call upon Him and accept the gift of forgiveness He is offering?" Rae didn't have to wait long for Liz to answer.

Without hesitation, through tears, Liz bowed her head and prayed a simple prayer. "God, I'm so sorry. I want what Grandmother had and what Rae and Allie have. I want you. I realize I'm a sinner and that Jesus died on the cross to pay for my sins. Please forgive me of my sins and come into my heart. Amen."

Allie, who had been listening at the den door, quietly came into the room and joined Liz and Rae in a sweet hug full of joy. Soon they were talking and laughing, happy that Liz was now a child of God. Hearing the commotion, her dad and brothers joined the celebration. Life for Liz would never be the same.

Chapter 7

With winter quickly departing, the small Aylett Baptist singles group joined the Southside group for a skiing trip to Massanutten, located outside of Harrisonburg about two hours west of Fredericksburg. Two vans full of skiers and one van loaded with skiing equipment and necessary clothes for skiing headed out early one Saturday morning in late February for a fun day in the snow. Some would ski while others planned to snowboard or snow tube down the mountain.

Allie had invited Liz, who was an avid skier, and Cayden made sure Faith was invited. Both women fit right in with the happy group as they set out for one last winter adventure. As the women chatted, Faith determined that Cayden was probably more on her level of novice skier and they became buddies, happy to trail along with the other snow tubers. However, by lunchtime, the two of them found their happy place in the clubhouse getting to know each other better. While they were cozy inside by a warm fireplace drinking coffee, Allie and Liz were loving every minute on the slopes. In fact, the guys were hard pressed to keep up with them.

At lunchtime, Daniel and Cayden sat by Liz in hopes of getting acquainted with her. Liz and Daniel had chatted that morning about living in Lake Caroline and she remembered meeting him on a couple of occasions. Recalling that Rae mentioned Daniel was a pastor, she decided to ask him about his church. As if he knew what she was thinking, Daniel smiled and spoke. "Allie's told us about your decision to accept Jesus as your Savior. While congratulations may sound a bit lame, it's appropriate because you've made the most important decision of your life. So congratulations, Liz!"

As happy tears rolled down her cheeks, she whispered, "Thanks, Daniel! I'm still overwhelmed with wonder and awe that God loves me so much and that He's forgiven all my sins. All this crying is rather new too."

Cayden joined the conversation with, "Oh, that overwhelming feeling of awe and the tears may never fade. In fact, I pray they never do."

"Have you considered a church to attend? I believe Rae mentioned you are a member of a church nearby, but we would love to have you visit Aylett Baptist. It's not far from where we live, the folks are wonderful, and I hear the pastor is okay too," Daniel added with a grin.

As conversation turned to leaving, Liz prayed for guidance on which church to visit the next day and decided to take Daniel up on his invitation. She would know at least five people there, and that was more than she knew at her present church. For the first time in her life, Liz was excited about attending church.

The ride home was interesting in that the seating arrangements had changed, with the more enthusiastic skiers riding in the same van so that they could continue discussing the adventures of the day. Brandon and Daniel had given up their seats so that Allie and Liz could ride in the van with Luke, Gil, and Joey. That, of course, meant they would ride in the second van with Cayden, Faith, and a few others. There were no objections at all to the change in seating for the ride home.

Liz was happy to find herself part of a group of single Christians. As she thought of how different her life was from just one month earlier, she closed her eyes and thanked God for making Himself known to her through two women she now called not just friends but sisters. Rae had taught her that once you accepted Christ, you were part of God's family, which meant other believers were her sisters and brothers. What a wonderful thing to belong to God's family!

The next morning Daniel was happy to see Liz walk through the front door of Aylett Baptist. As he excused himself from a conversation with Mr. Dean, he went to welcome her but was glad to see that Brandon, Faith, Gil, and Joey had already formed a great welcoming committee. It was amazing to watch his church family grow and interact with each other.

He thanked God for the special bonds being made and was especially glad to recognize real spiritual growth in many in the singles group. Brandon was a big encouragement to the others, and Daniel saw in him the potential for a leader for the group. He, Brandon, Gil, and Joey were spending more time together and he found their support particularly uplifting. Sometimes,

Luke joined them for a basketball game or a round of golf, which added to the sweet comradery they enjoyed. Gil and Brandon now sang in the choir and Joey often played either the violin or guitar as special music. Brandon had also taken an interest in helping with the new audiovisual equipment recently installed. With a thankful heart, Daniel found himself saying Cayden's favorite quote, "God is good all the time and all the time God is good!"

March blew in like the proverbial lion and two days later Ila and Phillip blew into town. The Feed My Sheep ministry was growing, and they were traveling almost nonstop with little time at home in Fredericksburg. Although Ila missed their little apartment and especially her friends, she wouldn't trade this whirlwind life of service to her Lord for anything. She could hardly believe in just two weeks she and Phillip would be celebrating their first wedding anniversary. Time really was flying but she was happy to look back over the past year and see the blessings God had so graciously bestowed on them and their ministry. It was exciting to think what the next year would hold for them.

With Ila home, it was time for a girls' night and Allie and Cayden were on it. They met at Cayden's apartment because it was larger than Ila's apartment and had only a small dog to occasionally interrupt. So much had happened over the last two months, which meant meeting early and staying late with lots of food to supplement endless conversation, laughter, and sometimes tears—the perfect recipe for a perfect girls' night!

"First, you have to tell me everything about the night Liz accepted Christ. Emails are good but hearing it will be better," Ila said while grabbing a handful of popcorn.

Allie was thrilled to oblige and Cayden shared her interactions with Liz during the trip to Massanutten. "I was happy when she joined our ski trip and glad to get to know her a little. Daniel invited her to services at Aylett Baptist and she's visited a couple of times. Not to change the subject, but I wanted to run something past you girls. Daniel and I would like to have a party at his house on March 16 to celebrate a certain couple's anniversary and their birthdays. It's also an excuse just to pull us all together for a fun, relaxed time before you guys leave again." Looking at Ila, she asked, "Will you still be here that weekend? Since March 17 is a Sunday, we thought you wouldn't mind us partying the day before."

Ila squealed at the mention of a party and Allie gave Cayden a high five. It seemed all were in agreement and the conversation quickly turned into a planning party. By the time Ila and Allie said their goodbyes and hugs were shared, there was nothing left to do but invite their friends and make the refreshments. Cayden couldn't wait to fill Daniel in on what would be their first party hosted together as a couple.

Since the weather promised to be unseasonably warm for mid-March, the party was planned as a cookout. Daniel manned the grill while the other guys gave advice on how to properly cook hamburgers and chicken. All side dishes and desserts were ready and the girls were happy to pretty much sit back, chat, and lend a hand as needed. When the afternoon turned cooler, a fire was built in the firepit and everyone brought their chairs up closer to enjoy the warmth not only from the fire but also from their sweet fellowship with friends, both old and new.

Liz was glad when Brandon and Faith showed up and she no longer felt like the only newcomer to the group. She was happy getting to know this new "family" of hers and enjoyed the easy way they discussed God as part of their everyday lives. Gil was fun to listen to as he talked about his small farm and plans he had to one day run a large farm. She had fun talking with Joey, especially about his love for music and his latest carpentry project. Allie had shared that Joey's fondest dream was to one day have his own shop, making and selling hand-crafted furniture. The more she learned about Allie's family, the more she liked them.

"Penny for your thoughts," Gil offered as he sat down in the chair next to her. "You have such a peaceful, contented look on your face that I hesitated to say anything. But I believe they're moving inside to play Pictionary and I thought you should be warned that this group can be more than a little competitive when it comes to games. Also, I'm one of the team captains and wanted to ask if you'd be on my team."

Surprised, Liz laughed and replied, happy that he had asked, "Of course I'll be on your team, but why in the world would you ask me? You can't have a clue whether or not I have an artistic bone in my body."

"Well, there's where you're wrong. Mom has mentioned several times about how you decorate your classroom, and I saw for myself some of the props and backdrops you created for the play. You're really talented and I am really not." Taking her hand to help her up, he added in a whisper, "You'll be my secret weapon!"

While Cayden got everything set up for Pictionary, Daniel went over the rules and announced the team captains, who then picked their teams. He then proceeded to warn everyone about "Killer Cayden," whose reputation was known far and wide for doing whatever was needed to win just short of actually cheating. Instead of defending herself, she graciously took a bow and thanked Daniel for the high praise before explaining to newcomers that he had given her that nickname after a rousing game of Pictionary at a Christmas party, adding with a wicked grin that her team still reigned supreme.

When it was time to call it a night, Allie slipped up to Cayden and put an arm around her waist. "This has been just what we all needed. You and Daniel throw a pretty great party. But maybe the next big party will be to make some type of important announcement." Ila walked up at just the right moment to hear Allie's comments and added her agreement. All Cayden could do was give them a dreamy smile and squeeze them tightly. She had filled them in on her and Daniel's Valentine dinner but omitted the part concerning their thoughts on the future. None of them knew what the next months would hold, but she knew one thing for sure: God had it under control and whatever happened would be according to His plan and in His timing. Of that, she was blessedly sure.

About a week later, while helping her mom make dinner, Allie was surprised when talk turned to some possible changes on the farm. Her dad and uncle had pretty much run the family farm as their parents had. So to hear they were considering changes was interesting, to say the least. Her dad always tried to keep up with new farming trends and often enjoyed taking classes on topics that particularly seemed to fit in with their type of farming, but to think of him considering some significant changes was surprising.

"The McIntree farm is going to come on the market soon. Your dad ran into Paddy McIntree last week at the co-op. His health is beginning to pose a problem for him to keep up with everything farming entails." Rae explained the situation as she finished the biscuits and placed the pan in the oven. "Your dad and Uncle James are thinking about buying it."

Allie's surprise was evident in her voice as she pointed out a very important fact. "But didn't Mr. McIntree change over to organic farming years ago? Would they keep it organic? Wouldn't that involve a lot of extra bookkeeping, etc., to keep the organic certification?"

"That's what's gotten your dad excited—the idea of organic farming. For a while now, he's been doing a lot of research and recognizes the benefits and the extra work, but he believes it will be more than worth it." Taking the biscuits out of the oven, she turned to Allie and shared a secret. "Your dad plans to ask Gil if he would manage the organic farm. It would be part of Blessed Acres but remain a separate entity legally in order to make things easier. What do you think of that? Do you think Gil would want to do it?"

Allie didn't have to consider her answer, "Of course, he would want to do it. In fact, it would fit right in with his dreams. But Mom, he would have to quit his job with the cable company. That's big!"

"Well, please pray for your dad and Uncle James as they make their plans and for guidance for Gil when he's asked to take part. Gil knows your dad might be interested in buying Paddy's farm, but he doesn't know he might very well be the determining factor."

Allie grinned cheekily as she replied, "Mum's the word, Mum! And I will be praying. Gil's dream of being a full-time farmer might be coming true, and that's exciting."

As Rae poured tea into glasses and Allie finished setting the table, Rae had one additional request. "I've prayed for mates for my children most of their lives and I'm trusting Him to provide that mate in His timing. As Gil makes this major life decision and takes on a huge responsibility, I'm praying for him harder than ever. Not every woman is cut out to be a farmer's wife, especially a *good* farmer's wife. None of the young ladies either of the boys have brought home to meet the family seem to fit the necessary description. So as you pray, please ask the Lord to prepare a young woman who has the desire and ability to love Gil and at least like farm life." Hearing Richard and her sons on the back porch, she brought the conversation to an end and hugged her daughter. It was lovely having a daughter who was also your sister-in-Christ!

Chapter 8

March went out like a lamb and everyone welcomed the signs of spring that were popping up in flower beds and in the budding trees. Spring was Allie's favorite time of year, especially on the farm where baby goats and calves could be seen playing in the fields along with some new kittens and a brand new litter of puppies. The cool mornings gave way to warmer days and softer breezes, and Allie just felt rejuvenated. Then there were the expected April showers that played a beautiful symphony on the tin roof of their old farmhouse. Her world was just about perfect and she was thankful for it.

Luke's parents also owned an older farmhouse on five acres in Stafford County. His dad and mom, Jeff and Teresa, enjoyed their little rural retreat after spending stressful days in their public jobs as accountant and paralegal, respectively. Although Luke had a nice townhouse in Fredericksburg not far from the academy, he still spent a lot of time at "home." As an only child, his parents welcomed him anytime he showed up to check on them or to just hang out with them, and of course to enjoy a good home-cooked meal.

When Luke asked how they would like to celebrate their thirtieth wedding anniversary, they were quick to let him know a nice meal at home with a few friends would be lovely. So he put a plan in motion for a simple but elegant dinner party. The caterer would cook, serve, and clean up after the meal. Guests would include Pastor Harwell and his wife Marietta, Don and Beth, and Ellen and Connor, which meant their large dining room table would be full except for one seat. That's when it dawned on him that he needed a date. Without missing a beat, he decided who to invite.

Allie was just getting in her car after work to meet up with Cayden at the gym when her phone rang. She was surprised to see Luke's name when she checked her phone. "Hey, Luke, how's it going?" Expecting him to ask her where one of her brothers was, she was surprised again when he asked if she would like to come to his parents' anniversary dinner. He had been sharing details of his plans with her and Cayden and it sounded like it would be a nice time, especially because she thought of his parents almost like family since she'd known them all her life. When she didn't answer immediately, he went on to explain that he'd just realized he needed another person to fill the table. Seeing no reason to decline, she accepted the invitation and asked if there was anything she could do to help, to which he offered thanks but assured her it was all under control.

Later, she mentioned the invitation to Cayden, who said how nice it was that she would be Luke's date for the dinner he was working so hard to pull together. At Cayden's use of the word "date," Allie began to wonder if Luke meant for it to be an actual date or if he just needed a pal to make up the numbers. She supposed it really didn't matter but yet somehow it did. Had Luke just asked her on a date?

He was having similar thoughts after talking to Allie. She was the only person he thought about when considering a date, but he rationalized that asking someone he knew so well made perfect sense. Then he realized that he had been thinking more about Allie lately—more than just old friends and more like someone it would be fun to really get to know. Happily surprised at this turn of events, he was looking forward to the dinner more than ever.

At church the following Sunday, Teresa and Rae had nursery duty together during Sunday school. Talk automatically led to Luke planning such a lovely dinner for his parents and then on to Luke inviting Allie. Both mothers happily agreed it was a date but wondered if their children knew it.

The following Saturday was Jeff and Teresa's anniversary, and they were excited for the dinner party planned for that evening. Luke had sent his mom off for a mani/pedi appointment while he finished up preparations. Since he had to be at the house to make sure last minute details were taken care of, he couldn't pick Allie up, but she assured him she didn't mind driving. She arrived a little early just in case he needed any assistance. When she rang the doorbell and he answered the door, he was taken aback at how lovely she looked. Gone was the Allie he'd grown up with, gone to camp with, and teased about her freckles and before him was a beautiful, poised young woman dressed for a formal dinner party. When she called his name a second time, he snapped back into the present and invited her in.

Allie had a similar experience when Luke answered the door in black trousers and a starched white shirt. His black hair, which was usually tousled and a little shaggy looking, was styled with just enough product to hold it in place. She thought he looked rather like a *GQ* model, and she liked it.

They quickly regained their equilibrium and made an effort to act casual. But they both knew something had just changed and they were looking forward to seeing exactly where it would lead. Tonight was going to be fun and, perhaps, rather interesting.

The caterer did a magnificent job, timing each course so that there was lots of time for talking and enjoying each other's company. After the meal, guests were invited into the den, where coffee and dessert would be served. The weather was perfect for leaving the windows open to welcome the warmer spring air, which set the tone for a relaxed time of conversation and enjoying the company of friends. Allie found herself sad at the thought of the evening coming to an end. She had enjoyed talking with all the guests but, particularly, with Luke. So much of the time they were together, her brothers or friends were part of their conversations, and it was lovely to quietly discuss topics more tailored to their interests. She had officially gone from wondering if this was a date to hoping it was.

Luke's thoughts were running along the same line as Allie's and he found himself wishing he had picked her up so that they would have the ride back to her house to continue talking. However, his duties as host took precedence and when the others left for home so did she. Realization hit him hard as he watched her drive away—he really, really liked Allie Lambert.

The next morning just before lunch break the school secretary came into Allie's class carrying a large white box with a familiar label on the top that read Paul's Bakery, which meant yummy goodies were inside. Allie quickly motioned for the grinning secretary to follow her into the hallway before asking, "Where did that come from? Did my mom drop it off or maybe one of the parents?" Possibilities ran through her head. Was today's date special in some way? Had she done something extra for one of the children lately? But nothing came to mind. Then she noticed a card sticking out of the box that read "Special treats for Miss Lambert's class because their teacher is a special treat." Still having no clue, she looked at the secretary, who seemed to be enjoying this way too much.

"A young man dropped it off," she offered. "I guess he could be old enough to be one of the parents but I've never laid eyes on him before, and I would remember because he was quite handsome."

The secretary was from Ladysmith and knew her family, meaning it wasn't one of her brothers. Stopping abruptly as her mind switched tracks, she wondered if it could have been Luke. With her heart beating a bit faster, she asked if the young man had black, sort of shaggy hair and if the secretary had possibly noticed what color or make car he was driving.

"That's a good way to describe his hair and he pulls the shaggy look off quite well, sort of like a younger Kurt Russell. I did notice his car because he pulled right up to the front door and because my sister has an Outback the same color blue." When she saw that Allie had solved the puzzle of the good-looking deliverer of bakery goods, she handed her the box and said as she walked away, "Hope you enjoy whatever's in that box as much as you seem to enjoy knowing who was sweet enough to give them."

Hurrying back into the classroom, she found her students sitting quietly but expectantly as they stared at the box. Finally, one of them asked what it was and if it was for them, and she assured them they would share the goodies after lunch. The card, however, was slipped safely into her purse. Finally, she knew without a doubt that last night was a date.

Allie couldn't wait to get to her car after school and call Luke to thank him. As she walked through the parking lot rummaging in her purse for the car keys, she didn't notice the man leaning against her car with his long legs crossed at the ankles until she was a few feet away. When she looked up and saw Luke, her heart missed a beat before picking back up at a much faster rate than usual. He was the first to speak, "Hello, Miss Lambert, how was your day?"

"Well, actually, Mr. Carson, it was quite lovely. In fact, one might say it was sweeter than most days." She unlocked the car and placed her purse and briefcase inside before leaning against the car next to him in a similar pose. "Thank you for your gift to me and to my students. The card had me scrambling to think who would say that about me and then I asked Beulah, our secretary, to describe the man who delivered the box. You'll be happy to know she was smitten by your good looks and that she could tell me the make, model, and color of your vehicle."

"So she thinks I'm good looking? But what do you think? Did she describe me correctly?" He pushed away from the car and turned to look directly at her as he spoke.

Unable to look away and feeling her face coloring, she simply said, "Yes."

He was surprised that she didn't banter back at him like she usually did, but he was happy with her response. Clearing his throat, he asked if she would like to have dinner with him. When she accepted his invitation, he started backing away, saying, "Okay, I'm leaving before you change your mind. I'll pick you up at six and we'll go to Mama Angelina's." He reached his car and was about to get in when he turned and added, "Thanks, Allie, for agreeing to a second date!"

Dating a guy that was close friends with your brothers was sometimes trying. Allie had dated a friend of theirs the year before, but he didn't live nearby and mingle with them on a regular basis. This was different because when Luke arrived to pick her up and Gil or Joey was around, they would forget he was there to see her and not them. On the other hand, it was fun that Luke was so comfortable with her family and that she was getting to know another side of him that even her brothers didn't know. The boy she'd known all her life and the girl he'd always known really weren't who they were today, and the more time they spent together the more they liked the grown-up versions of Luke and Allie.

In May, Cayden and Allie began planning a girls' road trip to Florida. The previous summer they had invited Marta to join them for a week sightseeing in North Carolina, Kentucky, and Tennessee. It was such fun that they decided to do it again only this time they would be driving down to St. Augustine, Florida, where Cayden's Grandma Phyllis had an apartment in a senior living community. Grandma was going to move in with Cayden's parents and needed someone to drive her to Virginia Beach because, according to her, there was no way she was getting on an airplane. She'd lived eighty-three years without flying through the air and didn't intend to start doing it at this late date.

As soon as school was out in early June, they would hit the road, stopping for a couple of days in Charleston, South Carolina, to break up the long drive. Charleston was one of Cayden's favorite places with so many beautiful historic homes and plantations, and the food was marvelous. Allie had always wanted to go, and she was excited for the opportunity to experience it with someone who knew a lot about the Lowcountry. Also, they were getting constant feedback from Daniel about what to do in Charleston since he had been born and raised there. His pages of information rivaled anything they could get from any tour book.

When Coral heard they were stopping in Charleston, she asked if she might tag along. Her sister, who lived ten minutes outside the city, had been begging her to come for a long visit and would be happy if Coral could hitch a ride down with them. Coral would then fly back at the end of her two-week visit. In fact, Coral's sister invited Cayden and Allie to stay with her the two nights they were stopping over on their way south. Her children would be away at church camp that week, which meant she had plenty of room. After Coral assured them her sister Ann would not offer if she didn't really want them to take her up on her offer, they accepted and looked forward to spending time with some of Coral's family.

Loving the beautiful spring weather, Daniel and Cayden took every opportunity to ride bikes, play tennis, or take their kayaks out on the river or Lake Caroline. They also fished a lot, something Cayden was learning to really enjoy, which made Daniel truly thankful. Now that Allie and Luke were dating, it was fun to invite them to join whatever plans were on for a Saturday. Of course, Buddy tagged along whenever possible.

In mid-May, Daniel began talking about hiking up Old Rag Mountain near Sperryville. The hike itself would take over six hours and was considered physically demanding, and the travel time to Sperryville from Aylett would be at least two and one-half hours there and another two and one-half hours back home, which meant a very long, physically demanding day. Daniel had hiked the mountain before and loved the challenge as well as the reward when you , reach the top and enjoy the panoramic view of God's beautiful creation. Those hardy enough to buy day tickets for the hike to join Daniel included Luke, Simon, Brandon, Gil, and Joey. Although Cayden would love to give it a try, she knew she wasn't quite ready to tackle it and she wasn't alone. None of the other women felt up to it, but they didn't want to be left out so they made plans to join the guys as far as Sperryville and then cross the mountain to visit Luray Caverns and shop and dine in Luray. In the end, Cayden, Allie, Coral, Liz, and Faith signed up for what they called "the sane and fun" part of the day's excursion. They rode up in two vans, hikers and shoppers in both vans until they reached Sperryville, where the hikers took a van and the shoppers took the other. Prayers were offered for safety before the group split up and Daniel reminded the ladies that cell phone reception would probably not be very effective. In fact, the guys all agreed to silence their phones during the hike so as not to get distracted or to distract others making the climb. Simon kissed his credit card goodbye before handing it to Coral, which made everyone laugh and broke any tension concerning the hike.

The hiker group returned home safe and sound, exhausted and happy from their day in the wilderness. While their wallets might have been a bit lighter than earlier in the day, the ladies agreed they'd made the right decision to sightsee and shop. However, several of them talked about tackling the hike the next time the opportunity arose.

Chapter 9

Cayden's brother Carter thought this day would never come—graduation from high school. He did have to admit, though, that his senior year had gone by rather quickly and that while he wouldn't miss the classes and some of the teachers, he would be sad to say goodbye to some of his classmates. In a large city like Virginia Beach, it was most likely he might never see the majority of them again, even guys he'd hung out with over the years. In the fall, he would start classes at Old Dominion University, and he was looking forward to spreading his wings to fly as he learned the ropes of campus life and sharing a dorm room.

His mom and dad weren't quite as ecstatic over their baby boy leaving home, even though the university was only about thirty minutes away. They thought it was hard when Cayden went off to college, but this seemed different since they would officially become empty nesters. But they'd gotten on board with Carter's plan and were actually very glad his plan included a college so close to home.

Graduation was Saturday morning at ten, and they were having a cookout afterward to celebrate his big day and the fact he was graduating in the top ten percent of his class. When Cayden and Daniel arrived Friday evening, several other family members were already there along with Carter's girlfriend Clarissa. It appeared a pre-graduation party was in full swing and they joined in the fun and with helping her mom in the kitchen.

When Cayden went into the kitchen to refill a bowl of chips and looked out the window, she noticed her mom sitting on a swing in the back yard slowly swinging back and forth. It was the first time she'd had a chance to talk to her mom alone since arriving, and she took advantage of what might be the only quiet opportunity they had to chat tonight or tomorrow.

Joining Meg on the swing, she took her hand and sat quietly as they slowly swayed back and forth in the still night. Other than noises filtering out to them from inside the house and the occasional car passing by, they were in their own bubble, and both women enjoyed the peace that ensued. Meg was first to break the silence, "You know I'm happy Carter's growing up and pursuing his path in life, but this is hard for me. Hey, I thought kindergarten was hard, remember?" Giving her girl a watery smile, she continued, "You seemed a bit more mature than Carter when you graduated, but then that was several years ago and I may be seeing it through rose colored glasses. Anyway, I have to get a grip because I will not spoil this very important day for him."

Cayden pressed Meg's hand and did the only thing she knew to do—pray. "Dear Heavenly Father, please help Mom and Dad as they see their baby boy graduate and begin this new, exciting chapter of his life. Keep Carter safe physically and spiritually, help him to make good choices, and please help him to reflect your glory in his daily walk. May he be a light in what can so often be a very dark world and help him flee temptations to follow the world instead of you. One last thing, Lord, please bless Mom and Dad as they enter a new and exciting chapter of their lives too. May they grow closer and enjoy time unfettered by the needs of two children, who love them and appreciate all the sacrifices they've made for them. Thank you, Father! In Jesus's name, Amen." As she prayed, Meg laid her head on Cayden's shoulder and wept quietly, but by the time Cayden finished praying, her eyes were clear and her smile bright.

"Thank you, my sweet girl. You are such a blessing. I'm fine now and ready to party. Guess we better get back in there and refill all the trays and bowls because I know that crew can eat." Standing up, she hugged her daughter and marveled at the beautiful, confident woman Cayden had become. As a way to let Cayden know she really was all right, she said what she'd said so many times over the years when they finished swinging, "Race ya!" and she took off running, with Cayden laughing and running alongside her.

Graduation went off with little or no drama. It was a really large graduating class, but the administration knew how to move it along quite efficiently. Afterward at the house, more photos were taken of the man of the hour showing off his diploma and then it was time to relax, eat, and have fun. Meg had it all arranged before they left for the ceremony, and they mostly just had to set everything out while Paul grilled the hamburgers and brats. When they sat down to eat and the blessing had been asked, Carter made a speech thanking everyone for coming and especially his mom and dad for, well, everything. Cayden was sad to leave the fun but reminded herself she'd be back in less than two weeks, bringing Grandma Phyllis with her.

Cayden, Allie, and Coral headed out on their girls' road trip early on a beautiful Friday morning in mid-June, full of plans and joy at the prospect of time away with good friends. They arrived at Ann's house in Mount Pleasant, South Carolina, midafternoon and were greeted with enthusiastic hugs. Ann, who looked so much like Coral, was a wonderful hostess, and her home was a beautiful, old, Lowcountry house with a large screened-in porch across the front. Shortly after she settled them in their rooms, they joined her on the porch where she served tea and delicious shortbread cookies that seemed to melt in your mouth. Allie found herself thinking maybe she'd stay with Coral at Ann's for the next two weeks.

"My husband Charles is an attorney with a large firm with offices in Charleston and Columbia. This morning he was called to a meeting at the state capitol and will be gone for several days. He asked me to apologize for his absence." Ann's slow southern drawl was as pleasant as the woman herself. "Usually, I'm at loose ends when he's not home, even when the children are here, but this time I'm excited because it will give me a chance to spend time with my favorite sister and my two new friends. Now I don't want to interfere with any plans you already have, but I hope you won't mind if I tag along."

Allie spoke up first, "Of course we don't mind. In fact, we're thrilled you can join us and maybe even show us some sights we'd miss otherwise. This is my first trip to Charleston and, in case you can't tell, I'm so excited." She realized she was sounding more wound up with each word and decided to just stop with the facts.

Ann thought for a minute and asked, "Have you made reservations for dinner? If not, that should be our first order of business. This time of year is busy around here and wait lists can be quite long." When the others indicated they had no reservations, she continued, "Well, if you don't mind, I think I know just the place to take you for a great taste of Lowcountry cooking."

Coral quickly discerned her sister's thinking and grinned. "I hope you mean where I think you mean. Do you think you can get a reservation?"

"Well, if the front desk can't help me, I can always call my friend Bess, the head chef. She's never failed me yet." Ann reassured Coral all would be well as she called the number programmed into her phone, which to Allie and Cayden meant this was going to be a really good restaurant. After asking about a reservation for six and being told it would be more like eight-fifteen, she asked if Bess was working. After a brief hold, Bess came on the line. "Bess, honey, it's Ann. We've got some girls from Virginia and my sweet Coral visiting and we need a table at six. Can you help?" And in less than a minute they had a table at what Coral called the best restaurant for southern food with lots of soul.

With Ann and Coral leading them, the girls had a wonderful time. Jestine's Kitchen was their first stop, and the food lived up to Coral's praise. Bess stopped by their table to welcome them and catch up with Coral for just a minute before needing to hurry back to the kitchen. The place was hopping and the girls understood why. When they mentioned dessert, both Ann and Coral recommended that although desserts there were great, they might want to wait and see if anything else interested them as they walked down Meeting Street to Market Street. Thankful for their advice, Allie and Cayden were happy indeed when they found a shop selling not only heavenly fudge but also amazing pralines. Remembering Daniel had mentioned that he loved a good praline, Cayden bought more than she probably should have but couldn't resist. They were so good.

Saturday started with a visit to Glazed Gourmet Donuts, where Ann and Coral insisted they try the Purple Goat donut, which was an instant favorite. It was a day of adventure, with tours of two plantations and shopping in City Market. Of course, Ann knew just where to shop and again led them to the best eateries in the city. Their trip was off to an awesome start, and it got even better on Sunday when they worshipped with Ann at her church on John's Island. They were sad to say goodbye to their hostess and to Coral after a wonderful seafood dinner, where Allie particularly liked the gumbo. They were heading on south to sightsee in Savannah that evening and all day Monday before traveling to Grandma Phyllis's.

Neither of the girls had visited Savannah, and both imagined it would be a lot like Charleston but found it had its own vibe and flair. Sunday night's dinner was a must at Lady & Sons, where they had made reservations thanks to Ann's suggestion. The restaurant was not far from their hotel so they walked, which it seemed everyone else was doing too. Again they enjoyed a delicious southern meal and were only a little disappointed they hadn't seen Paula Deen or one of her sons.

Monday morning they grabbed the tour book and set out walking. They'd made reservations for a carriage ride, which was quite a lot of fun while also being very informative. By dinnertime, they were ready to do absolutely nothing except order a pizza and watch television. Savannah had been great and tomorrow they would travel on to St. Augustine, where Grandma would be waiting for them, eager to show them some of the sights in her town.

When plans were finalized for Grandma moving to Virginia, she had shipped everything except what she would need for a few nights, which fit in two suitcases. Since Cayden and Allie had done some serious shopping in Charleston and Savannah, it was a good thing Grandma traveled lightly. When Cayden packed them in the car Wednesday morning and asked if she was ready to go, she was surprised to see tears in Grandma's eyes.

"You know I've lived here since just after your Grandpa died. In that almost ten years, I've met a lot of people, some in relatively good shape and others not so good. I've enjoyed some great neighbors and spent time in Bible study and prayers with precious friends. Sometimes, I wearied over the years at the number of funerals, but I've always thanked the Lord for having this place for me. My prayer has been and will always be that I reflect His glory. I told my close friends goodbye already and I will miss them, of course, but I am truly looking forward to being with your mom and dad and Carter." Taking a last look around, she placed her key on the kitchen counter and moved toward the door as she added, "Right now, I'm looking forward to spending time on the road with two sweet girls. Let's get this girls' road trip back on the road." And with that, they were off.

In order to make the trip less taxing for Grandma, the girls planned to spend two nights in Olanta, South Carolina, which wasn't far from Florence and was where Grandma's best friend, Aunt Ruth, lived. When Grandma mentioned they would be coming by for a visit, Aunt Ruth insisted they stay with her. So they stayed Wednesday and Thursday nights enjoying Aunt Ruth's southern hospitality. Thursday, the girls went adventuring to see what they might find to do while the older ladies enjoyed a sweet time of catching up with each other.

After a hearty breakfast Friday morning, the three "girls" continued their road trip toward Virginia Beach. As they traveled north on I-95, they sang favorite hymns and listened to stories of what Grandma termed "the good ol' days." Allie shared information about her family and their farm and Cayden updated Grandma on what was new in her life. Around noon, someone mentioned stopping for lunch and Allie groaned. "While I admit I'm hungry and we need to eat, I declare once I get back home I might have to buy a new wardrobe!" Everyone agreed and decided to stop where they might order salads. Cayden knew that was probably a good idea because she knew her mother would have a great dinner waiting when they reached home.

Allie and Cayden were glad to deliver Grandma safely to her daughter's arms later that day and to unload their suitcases one last time before arriving home on Sunday. Saturday was just plain, good fun with Grandma, Cayden's mom and dad, and Carter. Sunday was also lovely as they worshipped with family and friends.

Allie especially enjoyed meeting Brandon's mother and father, and they enjoyed putting a face to her name. They also recalled that she was sister to Gil and Joey, who Brandon seemed to be great pals with. "Next time you're in Glen Allen to visit Brandon, be sure to give me a call so we can get you out to the farm for a meal. I know Mom, Dad, and the boys would love to meet you."

After another fine meal, this time at Longhorn Steakhouse, the girls set off for home. Allie popped in a Laura Story CD and turned up the volume. "Home, James, and don't worry about the speed! I'm ready to sleep in my own bed and see my family," Allie joked, but the sentiment was real.

Rae was also happy to have her family back together under the same roof for a late supper after church that evening and to hear all about Allie's adventures. It made her heart sing to see her precious girl so animated as she regaled them with stories about each leg of their journey and all the new dishes she'd tried along the way. As she looked around the table, she could see the others were just as enthralled by the girl who had been their bright spot her entire life. When Richard looked at her and winked, it was almost her undoing. How could one woman be so blessed? The answer, of course, was simple— because she had a heavenly Father who loved her and who enjoyed blessing his daughter.

While the girls were on their road trip, Daniel and Luke were busy at a Christian youth camp near Smithfield. When Simon had called asking Daniel if he had any teens planning to attend the camp and if he would like to combine their groups for travel purposes, he was grateful for Simon's kind offer. Daniel was thrilled to have three teens from his church going to camp, and he was excited about preaching during two chapel services as well as being a counselor. Luke was also a camp counselor and would be driving the Southside bus taking their group. Daniel would meet them with his teens at McDonalds in Glen Allen, where they would grab a quick breakfast and travel south for a couple of hours to the camp. The week was packed with Bible lessons in the mornings and sermons in the evenings, along with lots of physical activities during the days. It was a happy but tired group that traveled home the following Saturday morning.

Because cell phones weren't allowed at camp, Daniel and Cayden hadn't had a proper conversation in almost a week. When they talked Saturday night, she suggested they get together after work Monday because she knew he had to be exhausted after a week of being responsible for teens. What she'd really wanted to say was, "Please come over after church tomorrow night."

He must have read her mind because he quickly stated, "Cayden, I haven't seen you in over a week and I don't want to wait. Is it okay if I come by after evening service tomorrow? I won't stay long because you've got to be tired too, but I need to see you."

"Of course, it's more than okay, you big goofball! I've got so much to tell you about our trip, and I can't wait to hear all about camp. I'll stop on my way home from church and pick up something for supper," she added, knowing neither of them would have eaten prior to services.

The next evening as they ate orange chicken and fried rice, they filled each other in on everything that had happened over the week. It really didn't matter what they talked about because they were satisfied just being together and enjoying each other's company. Daniel realized it was time to go when Cayden stifled several yawns. When she protested, he said, "Okay, let's each say the one thing that stands out as a highlight for the week. You go first."

Without hesitation, she said, "Well, the true highlight was when you walked through my door earlier. I did not realize how much I would miss you." She grinned at him and then furrowed her brow as she thought back over her travels. "I guess spending that kind of time with Grandma was the real highlight. Don't get me wrong, Allie and I had a blast and getting to meet Ann and spend time with her and Coral was so cool. The time with Grandma was different from any other time with her because she really was just one of us girls, having fun, sharing life stories, and talking about our love for the Lord. Maybe that was the biggest thing—enjoying her as not just my grandmother but as a sister-in-Christ. I wouldn't trade it for anything and having Allie enjoy it too just made it all the sweeter."

Taking a second to gently wipe a tear from her face, Daniel replied without having to think about his answer. "Actually, I had three highlights because I got to lead three teen boys to Christ. After service Monday night, one of my teens, Roy, answered the altar call and I explained how he could know Jesus as his own personal Savior. Then, Tuesday after lunch, Pete, one of the boys from Southside, found me and asked me to pray with him. He understood what he needed to do and just needed someone to talk him through it. On Friday, we had a campfire service with time for anyone to give their testimony. While someone else was saying how much they had learned at camp, Mr. Dean's grandson Jason came up behind me and tapped me on the shoulder. There stood this sixteen-year-old football team captain almost sobbing too hard to speak. I took him back to the empty chapel and walked him through scriptures explaining why he needed Christ and how to accept Christ's free gift of love and redemption. He had questions and I took my time answering each one to make sure he fully understood. By the time he prayed asking Christ to forgive him and save him from his sins, we were both blubbering like little babies." He stopped to wipe away his own tears before continuing, "God is so loving and kind to allow me to have a part in those boys coming to know Him. Cayden, their lives are changed forever all because of Christ." He stood and pulled Cayden close as he offered a sweet prayer of thankfulness and praise.

About that same time, Buddy reminded them he was still around and needed a bit of attention. They took him for a short walk in the soft, summer night and reveled in the fact that the God who created the very stars above loved them enough to bring them together and to shower them with blessings beyond their understanding.

Chapter 10

At breakfast the next morning, Allie asked if Rae had heard from Liz lately. "Yep, she stopped by last Wednesday all excited about a class she's registered for that helps teachers understand how best to effectively help students who know little or no English. It was such a joy to see the girl excited like that. She's come a long way since she asked Jesus into her heart and life." When she saw Allie sit up a bit straighter with a look of interest her mother knew so well, she added, "Liz thought you might like to check it out too. It starts next Monday and runs for two weeks."

"I don't really have anything else planned and it would surely benefit me to get a handle on what to do that's best while not totally disrupting the rest of the class. When that happened last year, I think I did okay but never felt sure how effective I was. Luckily, I had a bright little girl who spoke Spanish very well and helped me when I couldn't remember how to say a particular word. Remember little Lolita? She was truly a Godsend and always so happy to help. I couldn't thank her parents enough for having taught their daughter their native tongue."

After finishing her breakfast and enjoying a second cup of coffee with her mom, Allie called Liz and invited her to come over for lunch, which Liz was more than happy to accept. While she didn't want to make a nuisance of herself by visiting Blessed Acres too much, she was always happy to spend time with the Lambert family.

When Liz arrived for lunch, she could tell something big was going on because it wasn't usual for everyone to be home on a weekday. With school out for the summer, she sometimes had to remember which day of the week it was, but she was pretty sure this was Monday and the whole Lambert clan, including Allie's Uncle James and Aunt Barbara, were on the back porch.

"Liz, you're just in time," Rae shouted. "Come on up and join the celebration!"

Liz didn't know what the celebration was all about, but she was happy to join them. The Lamberts were a happy bunch but not usually given to big displays of emotion. However, from the looks on James's and Richard's faces, it had to be pretty big news because they were practically beaming and slapping each other on the back. Gil looked about as happy as any person she'd ever seen, with a big grin and his blue eyes twinkling.

Allie pulled her up the steps and began explaining. "They did it! Dad and Uncle James just got back from signing the papers." Not knowing exactly what papers Allie was referring to, Liz was more confused than ever. Allie apologized and tried again, "Sorry, I didn't know if Mom had told you what they've been working on lately. They've bought the McIntree farm!"

"Congratulations!" she said while shaking hands with James and Richard. "That's big news. Sorry, if I sound clueless, but where is the McIntree farm? Will you raise the same crops and cattle like you do on Blessed Acres?"

While she expected Richard to answer, she was surprised when Gil began explaining. "Mr. McIntree has been organic farming for a while now and we plan to keep it an organic farm. That's a big change for us, but it will be good in a lot of ways. We'll take you over and show you where it is."

Unable to stay quiet, Allie happily added, "And guess who the manager of that farm will be?" When Liz could only stand there looking like a deer in the headlights because she had no idea how to answer, Allie laughed and clued her in. "Gil! Gil is going to manage the McIntree farm. No, let me correct that—Gil will be manager of Blessed Acres II!"

Now, all the excitement made sense. Not only was their farm growing, it was also investing in something new that would surely be more lucrative. Then a couple of thoughts popped into her head, making her ask, "Two things. First, won't organic farming be a lot of extra work with a huge learning curve?" She turned to Gil for the second question, "And does that mean you're quitting your job?"

"Yes, to both questions," Gil replied, "and I'm thrilled!" Without thinking, he took her by the hand and twirled her around. "This is going to be a wonderful challenge, which Dad and Uncle James think I'm ready for and so do I."

The celebration moved inside and continued through lunch. Liz helped Allie in the kitchen while Rae and Barbara joined the guys, adding to the conversation and plans for this new venture. Again, Liz was enthralled watching everyone happily enjoying each other while discussing their family business because it was so different from anything she'd ever known.

During lunch, Barbara shared something she'd been considering all morning. Usually the quiet, sometimes reserved member of the group, they were surprised when she tapped her fork on her glass, stood up, and declared with authority, "We're going to have a party to celebrate such an important family milestone! When we look back on this day years from now, I believe we'll recognize it for the milestone it is in the history and success of Blessed Acres." When her proclamation was met with total silence, she sat back down, sure she had misread the situation. But then the whole family began chattering in agreement and questions started flying. A party was just the thing and the Lamberts knew how to throw one heck of a grand party!

The date was set for the Fourth of July. An invitation list was quickly sketched out including family, neighbors, and church family from both Southside and Aylett. Instead of doing all the cooking, they decided to go all out and hire a caterer friend who specialized in putting on an impressive southern barbecue. Since the main details were quickly decided, the guys moved into the den to happily talk farm business, and the ladies continued bouncing ideas back and forth for things like decorating and entertainment. And Liz was glad to be included.

With July 4 right around the corner, assignments were quickly made with a plan to meet back that evening to report successes and regroup where necessary. Allie and Liz were assigned the task of creating the invitation and sending it to the printshop in town for a quick turnaround. They were also delegated to gather addresses and create labels so that the invitations would go into the mail possibly as early as the next evening. Barbara went home with her to-do list, which included procuring the caterer and contacting the rental company for tables, chairs, and at least two large tents. Rae, who was known for her expertise in planning party entertainment, was brainstorming for the best games for children and adults.

When they could catch a breath, the girls sat out on the porch with iced tea and Liz filled Allie in on the seminar that would begin the following week. She pulled a brochure out of her purse and shared the highlights with Allie, who was growing more interested in attending. As they discussed their experiences with helping students whose first language was not English, Allie decided to register if it wasn't too late. Liz grinned at her sheepishly and informed her she was already registered. "I knew you'd be interested and didn't want you to miss out, so I added you to the registration sheet. Plus, with a second person, my class fee was a little less, which just made sense."

Allie laughed at her friend's logic before saying, "You think just like me, spending money to save money! Thanks for thinking of me. Don't let me forget to write you a check when we go inside. I truly believe the lessons will be helpful." Looking across to where Liz sat at ease with her head leaned back on the chair cushion and her eyes closed, Allie could hardly recognize the woman who just months ago would not have done something nice to help her but who might have gone out of her way to cause her trouble. God's grace was something she cherished and tried not to take for granted, but it still amazed her when she saw it at work in someone else.

The group met back for pizza and subs that evening and reported where they were on their assignments. Allie had typed the address labels and Liz would pick the invitations up the following morning. She and Allie would get them ready to mail and take them to the post office. Allie also volunteered to send a save-the-date email to as many as possible telling them to watch the mail for the actual invitation. Barbara had been happily surprised that the caterer was available and was even happier to report they were now booked for their party. She'd had to call around to procure the necessary tents, tables, and chairs but that was done too. Rae pulled out a list of games for the children and entertainment ideas for the adults. As she read out the list, the guys recognized that they would be needed to help with things like fishing contests and four-wheeler races. Rae would come up with a roster of activities and assign people to be in charge as needed.

Allie added something she'd forgotten to share earlier, "Luke said to be sure and include him in any way he can help." When they all just rolled their eyes and grinned at her, she said in her most bored teenage voice, "What's the big deal? It's just Luke." To which, they all laughed and made suitable comments about what they were seeing grow into more than "just Luke."

The Sunday after receiving her invitation to the Lambert's party, Faith was helping Brandon in the sound booth before services and asked him how to get to the farm. Brandon was glad to write a simple map showing the few turns necessary from Aylett to Ladysmith. After church, he found her in the office and asked what her plans were for lunch. When she mentioned being on her own since her aunt was out of town, he nonchalantly asked if she wanted to join him at a nearby diner and was happy to hear her say yes.

Over lunch, they talked about things going on at church and Faith couldn't conceal her excitement over being invited to the party. "It really makes me feel like part of the group. Being new to the area, I haven't met many people yet, so it means a lot and sort of makes me feel accepted." She had stumbled for a second on the right word but decided that accepted pretty much summed up how she felt.

Brandon looked at her before nodding and adding his own appreciation of being accepted. "I've been in the area a while but haven't really gone out of my way to make friends because it seemed like work always was most important. It wasn't until I was back home last year and reconnected with Cayden that I realized how nice it was to have a friend to do something as simple as play tennis with and just chat about important and unimportant things. Since I decided to put myself out there and open up to meeting people, I've joined Aylett Baptist and made friends. Thanks to Cayden, I have friends at our church and Southside. But you know what's the best thing? I'm closer to God than ever before in my life."

Faith had stopped eating and sat watching the expressions that flitted across Brandon's face as he recounted his recent journey to where he was that day. When he mentioned a closer walk with the Lord, she chimed in, "Me too! I like the independence I have since moving here and, while it can be a bit scary sometimes having to feel my way along in a new place and new job, it's kind of exhilarating. And what's cool is that I've found a new desire for reading my Bible and talking to the Lord. Part of that can be attributed to Pastor Daniel's preaching and his encouragement to be an active child of God and not just a Christian who never takes the time to really get to know Him."

Their conversation continued in an easy manner as they finished up their dessert. Brandon had been considering something for a while and thought the timing was right to ask Faith a question. "You were asking about directions to the farm earlier. Would you like to go with me? I could pick you up that morning and we'll stay as long as you like. If the party ends around dinnertime, we can stop at one of my favorite restaurants in Glen Allen to grab a bite." There he'd said it. Now to see how she answered.

Only a little surprised at his invitation, Faith quickly answered, "That would be lovely, Brandon. Just let me know what time to be ready." She smiled when he seemed to let out a small breath. How about that? She had a date!

Blessed Acres was a beehive of activity the day prior to the party. Workers and volunteers came throughout the day to help with setup and last-minute preparations.

Liz and Gil sat down at the kitchen table with cups of coffee and some of Rae's scones to finalize plans for the fishing contests. James, the self-proclaimed fishing champion of the family, had drawn up the rules. For the morning children's contest, there would be two prizes—one for the child catching the largest fish and the other for whoever caught the most fish. Parents would be allowed only to help their children bait a hook and remove a fish from a hook. The afternoon adult contest would be solely for the largest fish caught in the one-hour time allotted. To make things fair across the board for both contests, only the bamboo poles provided could be used with nightcrawlers as bait. Gil and Liz would serve as scorekeepers and judges.

As they finished up, Liz decided to have a bit of fun by saying, "You know, I've always been pretty good at fishing. In fact, my brothers would get miffed when I caught more than they did, but my dad was proud to call me his little fishing buddy. Do you fish much, Gil?"

James, who had just walked in the back door, stopped to listen to what sounded like an interesting conversation because he knew how proud Gil was when it came to his fishing abilities. He wasn't disappointed when Gil took the bait Liz had so easily thrown out there for him. "Of course, as often as I get a chance I'm wetting a hook in our ponds, or over at Lake Caroline, or in the river. I imagine your daddy had to bait the hook for you just like we did for Allie." The last bit was added because he had seen Allie and Luke join James in the doorway. But before Allie could set the record straight that she had always baited her own hook, Liz sighed and calmly replied.

"Nope, in fact, I always volunteered to dig for the earthworms. So, Mr. Lambert, what say we have a little contest of our own?" Liz looked around the room that was now filling up with more family and friends. "Let's go fishing and see who catches the most fish in one hour."

Not one to back down from a challenge and secretly enjoying their banter, Gil agreed. "But what does the winner get? I mean, what's a contest without a prize?" Cocking his head to one side and rubbing his chin as if in deep thought, he suddenly sat up straight and snapped his fingers. "I've got it! Loser washes winner's car. Are you up for it?" He looked around the room with a cocky air as if he'd already won and the little lady would have to wash his always dirty farm truck.

"Why such a wimpy prize? Afraid you'll lose? How about loser washes my car each week for a month?" Liz knew she'd struck a nerve.

"You're on, and don't think I didn't see what you did there saying 'my car.' I'll get my fishing gear, and we'll fish right after supper. Oh, and if you don't have any gear, I'll be happy to share." Gil was now enjoying this way too much because he knew just where the fish would be biting at any given time of day. If this woman thought she could come to his home and out-fish him in his own pond, she had another think coming.

Just as he started to stand, James cleared his throat and interjected, "Now, Gil, that wouldn't be very fair for Liz would it? I mean, after all, you have home team advantage fishing in a pond you know like the back of your hand. So I'll draw up a map of the pond and divide it into numbered sections. Then you'll each draw which section you have to start fishing in at exactly six this evening. After that, Liz, you're on your own, but I've tried to even it up a bit. Oh, and you'll be using the same bamboo poles we'll be using tomorrow." He was full out grinning now because Gil wasn't quite as cocky as he'd been a minute earlier. Seeing that everyone was enjoying the show, he added, "And there's one more rule concerning smack talk and this goes for both of you and all spectators." He stopped again and looked around with a serious, I-mean-business expression before adding, "The more smack talk, the better!"

Everyone got back to work, but there was definitely an air of anticipation to see who would be washing whose car for a month. After supper, with work done and fishing on their minds, Joey hooked up the hay wagon and drove them up to what they called the big pond. James held the drawing to see where the contestants would start fishing, and it was off. Barbara, who was the official timekeeper and scorekeeper, announced scores every fifteen minutes. First, Gil was ahead by one, then Liz had him by two, and with only fifteen minutes left to go, they were tied. As her timer chimed the hour was up, Barbara proudly stood and announced the winner. "I hereby declare Liz the winner of this hard fought competition by one fish!"

Amid applause and general revelry, Liz took a bow and then curtsied before presenting Gil with a spare key to her Prius and saying in a saccharine sweet voice, "I'll let you know what day works best for you to come by to wash my car." Gil accepted it with a gracious bow and took the ribbing that followed like a man. He had really enjoyed spending time with Liz and getting to know her, even if it meant being out-fished by a girl!

Party day dawned clear and bright and temperatures were only supposed to reach a high of eighty-two degrees, mild for early July in their area. Guests were expected to arrive beginning around ten, with lunch at noon, and various forms of entertainment throughout the day until the last person left well after dark. They expected pretty much everyone invited would show up at some time during the day along with some that weren't actually invited but had heard through the grapevine that the Lamberts were throwing a party and thought no one would mind if they joined in the festivities.

Luke, Liz, Daniel, and Cayden showed up bright and early to help with last-minute details and to enjoy the huge breakfast Rae was cooking. Barbara made sure no one lingered overly long over breakfast so that she could have everything ready when the caterer arrived. His crew would take over the kitchen and the back porch. She also put them to work filling several really large coolers with ice, bottles of water, sodas, and juice boxes. The coolers were then taken by golf cart to specified areas on the farm where they would be handy for guests throughout the day. She had also paid three boys from church to check the coolers regularly and refill them as necessary, which meant they got to drive golf carts and have fun while getting paid for it—a win-win situation for everybody.

Blessed Acres was looking like a shiny new penny thanks to Rae's efforts working with the farm employees to mow lawns, weed flowerbeds, power wash the house, and give the rail fencing along the long driveway a fresh coat of paint. Richard had overseen a similar process at Blessed Acres II, readying it for the ribbon cutting and dedication ceremony planned for after lunch.

Joey was in charge of music, and he had recruited musician friends to play off and on during the day. He had set up square hay bales around the big barn closest to the house so that he could open the barn doors and have a stage of sorts and guests would have bales for seating. Barbara took charge of making sure the caterer had everything in hand and helped Rae with the adult games, while Luke and Allie worked with the children's games. Richard and James happily accompanied guests over to Blessed Acres II and explained their plans for the new organic farm. Daniel and Cayden were assigned as floaters, helping wherever help was needed. After Rae was sure everyone knew their assignments, she had one last thing to say, "And be sure to have fun!"

Richard was glad that Rae loved planning events and knew she would do a wonderful job, but there was one detail he wanted to take care of as a surprise for everyone but especially for her. At eight-thirty that evening, just as folks were winding down and enjoying Joey and friends' music, fireworks began going off nearby. He watched Rae looking around trying to figure out which neighbor was responsible as everyone else was oohing and aahing at the beautiful displays of light and color. After just a few minutes, she narrowed her eyes, looked directly into his, and quietly asked, "Are those fireworks coming from the McIntree farm?"

"Nope, they're coming from Blessed Acres II," he replied matter of factly. "I wanted to do something special for you, sweetheart, and thought this might be something to top off a special day for our family that you've worked so hard arranging."

When she just smiled and laid her head on his shoulder, he knew he'd done well. His earnest, beautiful, caring, hardworking wife accepted his gift and let him know it pleased her. What more could he want? Nothing.

As parties go, this one was the best ever on Blessed Acres. Guests left having eaten, played, and relaxed, all while celebrating their friends' good news and Independence Day in grand fashion. Walking into her kitchen, Rae was thrilled to find it all in order, which meant she could do the one thing she wanted more than anything to do—sit down in her recliner and put her feet up. Soon she was joined by her husband and children and they spent time discussing the different aspects of their day. The photographer they'd hired promised to get the photos and videos to them early the following week. But for now, they didn't need them to relive the highlights of this momentous occasion. It was better just listening to each of them as they talked, drawing word pictures of the day's events, and laughed, happy to be together.

Chapter 11

July also held a big milestone for Daniel when all his scrimping and saving over the years was rewarded with something he'd wanted for what seemed like most of his life. He was now the proud owner of a shiny new boat that was good for fishing, skiing, or tubing. His excitement was almost palpable when he and Cayden put it in the water for the first time. He didn't even give a thought to loading up all his fishing gear because all he wanted to do was to take it out on the lake and open it up. For years, he'd enjoyed his kayak and jon boat, but his heart had been set on something a bit more powerful and fun, and it didn't hurt that it was pretty snazzy to look at. It had lots of bells and whistles, and he couldn't wait to find out how to use them all.

Shaking her head at his boyish grin, Cayden congratulated him, "Oh, Daniel, you're going to enjoy this so much and you deserve it. Saving for something since you were a boy delivering newspapers and then actually getting it is a huge success. It sure is pretty."

"Pretty? Is that the best you can do? Come on, Cayden, you have to admit she's gorgeous. Just look at that candy red hull sparkling in the sunlight." When Cayden only laughed, he went on almost drooling, "Don't you agree she's so much more than pretty? I can't wait for the guys to see it, and my parents are going to flip out. There's some skiing in our future, Cayden girl! Just wait until we're at Lake Anna next month with my family." Captain Daniel was definitely enthralled with this new "she" in his life.

After a while, Cayden reminded him she had an appointment and would need to get back to the dock. "Allie should be waiting for me so that you can continue playing with your wonderful new toy."

As they pulled up to the dock, Daniel came back to earth and noticed some familiar cars in the parking lot. Then he saw people jumping up and down, whistling, and shouting and he realized it was Luke, Joey, Gil, and Brandon making all the noise while Allie just shook her head with a "boys will be boys" look on her face. As they helped secure the boat, Daniel asked Cayden what was going on and she gave him the sweetest gift.

"Well, I knew you'd want the guys to see your new boat and Allie told me how desperate they were to check it out. So she and I are going to do some shopping while you all inspect every inch, bell, whistle, button, and thing-a-ma-jiggy on your boat. Us girls will have our own fun, some dinner, and then she'll drop me at home." Allie came up and offered her congratulations before whisking Cayden away, leaving the menfolk as they boarded Daniel's new pride and joy for the first time.

Brandon had let Faith in on the secret Cayden had planned for the guys to be in on Daniel's big day. She was really glad he was making such great friends and even happier that they were getting closer. He had taken to calling her most evenings since the Lambert's big party, and she enjoyed chatting and learning more about him. Her day at work had been hectic and she was ready to get home and relax. Her job as a customer services consultant at a large car dealership in Glen Allen was something she enjoyed for the most part, and she really liked working from home four days and going into the office only once a week. Deciding to take secondary roads instead of getting on what most people called an interstate, but she called a raceway, she decided to stop at a park where she and Aunt Georgia had taken a walk recently. She joined a dozen or more people taking advantage of the cooler evening temperatures while getting in some exercise.

She'd done a lot of walking at a park similar to this one back home and that's when she did her best thinking and praying. It was just sort of natural to talk to God as she took in the beauty of his creation and let His peace soothe her spirit. As she walked along thanking God for all the blessings in her life, He reminded of something she'd asked Him two years earlier and she hadn't really thought a lot about since. But now He was showing her that He had answered her request, and the significance of it stopped her dead in her tracks. Thankful there was a bench nearby, she sat down as tears began flowing down her face.

Faith hadn't dated a lot of guys in her twenty-five years and, as a Christian woman, it seemed to get harder and harder to find a godly man to even consider dating. Two years earlier, she had met a guy at church who professed to love the Lord and from all outward appearances that was true. However, after dating for three months, Faith began to see things in his life that told a different story and she broke it off, but not without some heartbreak. She'd thought he might actually be the man God had for her, and her disillusionment was hard to overcome. So on a day a lot like that day, she had taken a walk and laid her hurt and anger at God's feet, asking Him for guidance going forward so that she would not date again until it was the man He wanted her to marry and live the rest of her life loving.

God had been faithful in those two years and no opportunities to date a Christian man had been given. That is, until Brandon asked her to join him for lunch a few Sundays ago and then invited her to go with him to the party. As clearly as if God had spoken aloud, she heard him plainly say, "Remember what you asked me two years ago?" Believing in God's mercy and grace and His faithfulness, she knew at that moment what perhaps only she and God knew—she was going to marry Brandon Printz.

Daniel's parents, Edward and Francine, decided to splurge and rent a large house on Lake Anna for the first week in August so they could vacation with their four children and their families. Their oldest, Julie, and her husband Jimmy would come in from Hampton and bring their precious grandbabies, Caleb and Marnie. Emily and Chad, who lived in New Market just two hours away in the Shenandoah Valley, would join them for the week but would have to pop back and forth to keep up with things at the antique shop they owned in Timberville. Their youngest daughter, Grace, was probably the most excited as she looked forward to being away from her office and just hanging out with her family. As an attorney in a small practice in Alexandria, she didn't get many chances to be away, and she planned to enjoy it to the max. When she found out that her baby brother had actually bought his dream boat and would be bringing it to the lake, her mind filled with many hours on the water relaxing and having fun fishing, skiing, or just soaking up the sun in relative peace.

Daniel arranged his schedule to spend Thursday through Saturday with them at the lake and to join them after work the other days. His parents had invited Cayden and she was going to come over each day after work but spend nights at home, which made it easier with work and with taking care of Buddy. Also, her parents were coming for a visit that same weekend so they could go to Aylett Baptist's annual picnic. Sad to miss all the fun, Grandma Phyllis would be staying home recuperating from a bad cold, with Carter for company.

Cayden and Daniel were excited for their parents to meet. After the picnic on Saturday, Meg and Paul would join them at the lake for dinner with his family; and the plan for Sunday was for everyone to attend Aylett Baptist, which would be yet another opportunity for the two families to bond as they worshipped the Lord.

The house they rented was on a cove with a small beach, boathouse, and dock. Daniel took his boat on the first day and left it for the family to use, making all of them quite happy. Caleb and Marnie particularly enjoyed the sliding board on the dock, which dumped them into the warm lake water. And, to be honest, the adults had fun sliding down it too.

Whoever built the house had thought of all the amenities to make a family vacation memorable. The three-story house had an entertainment room, game room, and a lovely den with books, comfortable chairs, and no other distractions except for the windows that looked out on the beautifully manicured lawn and the sparkling lake. The patio with grill and casual dining and the second-floor deck with more seating were used more than any other area. Francine's motto that everyone agreed with was to spend as little time in the kitchen as possible that week. Thankful that the area had some restaurants with delivery, they found themselves cooking only if someone actually wanted to cook.

Emily talked her sisters into joining her for a day of shopping in Fredericksburg, where they spent most of their time in old downtown. Emily particularly enjoyed the antique shops, while Grace had fun in the vintage clothes and jewelry stores. Julie was happy to be out with her sisters and taking time to look through clothes her size instead of Marnie's or Caleb's. She loved her children more than anything but she sometimes actually yearned for adult company, and she was soaking up every minute of it.

The guys seemed mainly to be attracted to Daniel's boat, taking it out each morning sometimes to fish and other times just to check out what was happening around the lake. When Caleb asked his mom what the boat's name was, Julie started forming a plan to memorialize this vacation, especially for Daniel.

When he and Cayden arrived that afternoon after work, Julie and her sisters had the plans in place and were ready to reveal them to their brother. Before dinner, she gathered everyone on the patio for what she called a big announcement. Daniel and Cayden seemed to be the only ones who didn't know what was going on, but they went along with the fun as Grace herded them all downstairs and outside.

Clearing her throat, Julie read from a piece of parchment paper in a clear, authoritative voice, "Hear ye, hear ye! It has come to the attention of this august group that the owner of the boat in yon lake has neglected to give it an official title. We find this oversight unacceptable and wish to correct the matter immediately."

When she stopped reading, Emily took up the obviously practiced speech, "Since the owner has not yet done his duty, we, his sisters, have gone to great lengths to search out some suitable names to bestow on such a noble vessel. As the official christening of this ship will commence promptly at seven, there is little time to waste for this group to vote on and approve the name that shall henceforth be recorded for posterity."

Standing and reading from her paper, Grace began to read the names they had come up with. Some were quite good and others downright hilarious. About halfway through the list, Daniel had to join the fun and raised a protest, "I beg your pardon, august group, but these names are not appropriate for such a fine vessel and I, as captain and master, must protest. Do you have others to suggest?"

"We do indeed, kind sir, and time is wasting as we near the time appointed for the christening. There are two more names, and these are the two we, your sisters, think best." Stopping to look around the group and to cue a drum roll, Grace offered the names amid laughter and many fingers drumming on the tabletop. "First, we offer 'Daniel's Fancy' for your consideration." When Daniel made a face that clearly said that was considered mediocre, she proclaimed the name they'd thought better than any other, "Trusting His Timing."

Caleb and Marnie looked around, not understanding why all of a sudden the adults had gone quiet. They had been allowed to make suggestions and came up with Donald Duck, Flipper, and Sparkles, all of which made perfect sense to them, and they didn't understand why the last name was interesting enough for Uncle Daniel to even consider. They exchanged a look that clearly said "guess you gotta be an adult."

Daniel looked at Cayden, who was smiling at him, while his sisters and mom were wiping tears from their eyes. Even his dad had taken out his handkerchief. Standing, he went to each sister and hugged her before turning to the group, clearing his voice, and saying, "We have a clear winner. The boat shall henceforth be known as 'Trusting His Timing.' Now, on to the christening!"

Never to do anything halfway, Julie, Grace, and Emily had set up a great christening celebration down at the dock complete with a bottle of sparkling white grape juice in netting, of course, to keep glass from going into the water, and a small spread of appetizers. When everyone started calling, "Speech, speech!" he obliged them with a short, heartfelt speech.

"Y'all know I've wanted a boat like this since I was seven years old and Uncle Harry took me out in his. Thanks to a lot of people's generosity," he said as he waved his hand around the group, "and hard work and saving as much as I could, God has given me this particular desire of my heart. There were a few times over the years that I had enough to buy a boat, but other more important things needed the money and I was glad to have the funds to take care of them as God led. Always, my prayer has been that He would grant my desire if it was in line with His will and when His timing was right. Well, He's answered my prayer and here she is. Dad, will you please pray for my new boat, Trusting His Timing?"

After Edward prayed, Daniel took the bottle of white grape juice and handed it to Cayden. "I believe it's traditional that a woman christens a boat. Will you do the honors?"

Surprised and touched, she took the bottle and cracked it against the bow of the boat, saying, "I hereby christen thee Trusting His Timing!" Bowing to the applause that followed, she grinned at Daniel. "So what are we going to call it for short? The same thing we've called it since you ordered it?"

Caleb piped up, "What have you been calling it? We've been just saying 'the boat' around here."

Cayden held up her hand to Caleb for a high five since that was exactly what they'd been calling it for the last few weeks. Daniel laughed and tousled Caleb's hair. "You're right, pal, we do all call it 'the boat' and I guess that's just fine. But I'll be having a nice graphic made up with her official name and putting it right here," he told him as he patted the front side of the boat.

Friday morning at breakfast, Daniel let his mom know not to plan on him and Cayden being with them for dinner. "I want to take my best girl out for a dinner cruise all on our own this evening. So we won't be joining you at the seafood house." When Francine asked if he needed any help with the dinner, he shared how he'd ordered a basket full of foods they liked from a Lake Anna eatery. "We haven't had much time for just the two of us in the last month. It seems like time has been booked with lots of stuff—mostly fun, so I'm not complaining—but some quiet time together would be nice. Plus, it might be the last chance to just take our time and tour around Lake Anna this week."

Francine knew her boy pretty well and could read the sincerity in his voice and in what he was saying, which meant she had to fight the overwhelming urge to pry and ask if this particular dinner had any special meaning. But she had learned with her three girls to bide her time and not push. He would share when he was ready. However, that didn't stop her from praying throughout the day for whatever God had in store for her son and Cayden. She knew her desires, but she set them aside as she ended each prayer with "thy will be done."

Daniel had spent part of the afternoon cleaning up the boat and stocking the cooler. He'd swung by the eatery and picked up the basket, happy with its contents, before coming back to dress for the evening. How cool it was to be taking his girl for a dinner cruise on his very own boat. As he dressed, he pondered again the name his sisters had known would resonate with him because it was so appropriate. He had been ready to order his boat at least twice over the past few years, but a special need in someone's life came up and he knew God was leading him to use the money to help them instead. He'd done it ungrudgingly and kept on putting money in his savings account as God provided.

When God called him to pastor at Aylett Baptist, he was happy to go where God was leading him, but he was surprised at the more than adequate salary they offered. Then, after being their pastor for six months, the church gave him a love offering that overflowed his heart and his savings account because once again he had enough to buy the boat. But he waited several months before again picking out the boat and traveling to Bass Pro Shops in Ashland to place the order. All the while, he prayed for God's leading, His timing, and His blessing where the money and the boat were concerned. When he felt only deep joy and thankfulness in his heart, he placed the order and now he was going to take the woman he loved for a ride in the boat he'd waited for so patiently.

As he drove to Cayden's apartment, his mind went to another area where trusting God's timing was more than crucial—his relationship with Cayden and plans for their life together. He prayed and knew she did too for God to lead them on the path He had for them, to open doors or close doors according to His will. God's hand was evident in each step they were following and His timing was perfect. Thinking led to praying, which led to joyful praising as he drove along. God was good all the time and all the time God was good!

After work, Cayden dropped by her apartment to freshen up, change clothes, and take care of Buddy. Don and Beth had invited her parents to be their guests for the weekend so that Cayden wouldn't have to give up her only bed, and she knew her parents were looking forward to visiting with them. Over the last two years, they had become good friends, even to the point that Don and Beth had spent a weekend or two in Virginia Beach with Meg and Paul. She would have a chance to see them when she took Buddy over before leaving for her date.

Daniel had told her his plans to have dinner on the boat so she dressed accordingly. She also factored in the fact it had been exactly one year today since their first official date, which meant taking a little extra care with her appearance. Taking just a minute, she mentally looked back over the year and all the blessings God had showered on them. She was humming as she scooped Buddy up and took him next door, where her parents and Don and Beth would spoil him while she was gone for the evening. Just as she was coming back out their front door, Daniel was getting out of his car, and she almost skipped to meet him. Tonight was going to be such fun!

Paul and Meg stood at the door watching their daughter walk toward the young man they believed God had chosen for her. Meg commented that they looked like an ad for a yacht club. Without coordinating, they each wore white with blue and red accents, which highlighted their summer tans. They had a classy, casual look and it suited them. As they watched their girl and her beau drive away, Meg wiped a tear of joy from her eyes as Paul gave her a sideways hug.

When they arrived at the lake house, they popped in for just a few minutes to say hello and grab the dinner basket. The family was going out to a local seafood restaurant they'd heard was excellent for dinner. While they all acted nonchalant, they couldn't wait to get to the restaurant and compare notes. Each had theories on what was happening in Daniel and Cayden's relationship and it was such fun bouncing ideas back and forth.

Daniel helped Cayden board the boat and stored their gear before steering it carefully out of the cove into the lake, while she relaxed in the seat next to his. She was even more beautiful than usual with the wind blowing through her auburn hair, which looked almost red in the late afternoon sunshine. He was struck anew at the fact this godly woman loved him and how very much he loved her.

Breaking into his reverie, she asked, "Captain, are we heading anywhere in particular or just adventuring on our first-ever dinner cruise?"

"I'll have you know I have a plan, and I have a particular place in mind where we'll anchor while we enjoy dinner. After that, we'll just go exploring. In fact, I was thinking maybe you'd like to take a turn at the wheel at some point." He was happy to see her look of agreement and anticipation. "We should be at our dinner destination in about ten minutes. How's that sound?"

"Marvelous! I admit I'm hungry and also curious about what's on the menu. As to me taking the wheel, that's a big yes! I've wanted to before, but there were always other people around and I'd rather my first excursion be just you and me. Plus, I never wanted to pry your fingers off the wheel!" Now, she was laughing and to him there was no sight more beautiful than his sweet Cayden.

True to his word, they anchored in a cove where they would have a lovely view of the sun going down over the lake and where there weren't many houses lining the shore. They started unpacking the basket and cooler, setting out one delectable surprise after another until they had a smorgasbord fit for a king.

When everything was ready and Cayden expected him to ask the blessing, he instead took her hands in his and shared his heart. "Cayden, you know I love you. This past year has been such a joy getting to know you better and watching our friendship grow into a deep, abiding love. Happy anniversary, sweetheart!"

Happy tears almost choked her, making it hard to speak, but she managed with, "I love you too, Daniel. God led me to you, and He's blessed us with a love that's strong and sure. This past year has gone by so fast, and I've enjoyed every minute of it because of you. I'm excited to spend the rest of our lives together loving Him and loving each other."

Daniel moved so that their heads were together as he prayed, "Dear Father, we come to you with such thankful hearts. Thankful that you love us, for our salvation through Christ, and the blessing of loving each other. We pray that we will always follow your lead and trust your timing in our lives. We ask that you bless our love and continue to work in our hearts to love you and each other more every day. Last, we ask that you bless this food and we thank you for providing it for us. Amen."

Dinner was exceptional, with incredible food and sweet conversation in a lovely setting. As the sun crept closer to the horizon, Daniel brought out jackets and Cayden brought out a white box filled with the most beautiful pastries. He had wondered what was in the box and had gotten his hand swatted when he tried to open it earlier.

"With me coming to visit with your family after work each day, I didn't have time to make anything, so I asked Ellen to pack us a goodie box. When I picked it up, she made me promise not to peek inside until we opened the box together." As she looked at the luscious delights, she saw a small white card tucked along the side of the box. "Oh, look, Daniel! She added a card."

Unable to read it through tears of joy, she handed it to Daniel, who read, "Dear Daniel and Cayden, I hope you enjoy these pastries as they were made with love just for you. Happy Anniversary! Love, Ellen."

Thinking there could be no better time than this happy moment, Daniel got down on one knee as he pulled a small box from his pocket and simply asked, "Cayden Dewitt, will you please marry me?"

Although she thought he might propose tonight, she was still surprised when he dropped to his knee. He was equally surprised when she jumped up, pulled him up with her, and hugged him tightly. "Yes, Daniel, I'll marry you!" she shouted and then remembered there was a box in his hand that she'd totally ignored. Pulling back far enough to see the box and its contents, she started bawling and laughing at the same time. Not surprised by her reaction, he took the ring and gently slid the beautiful oval diamond solitaire ring onto her finger. She would spend a lot of time just looking at it later, but for now she was enthralled with the fact she and Daniel were going to get married and that was enough to fill her heart and mind for quite some time.

As promised, Daniel turned the wheel over to her and instructed her as she steered back out into the lake. After just a few minutes, she felt she had the hang of it, and he stepped back as she confidently increased speed until they were skimming along the water enjoying the early evening and the beautiful scenery. Houses of all shapes and sizes dotted the shoreline, and it was fun watching as lights began coming on in them and imagining the people who lived there. Birds flew past back to their nesting places, preparing for night, while some continued fishing for their last meal of the day. A few night birds joined them, swooping here and there doing a sort of twilight dance. They took this all in while wrapped in a sweet cocoon of pure joy knowing they were going to spend the rest of their lives loving each other and thrilling at the wonderful adventures that awaited them.

When they were almost back to their dock, Daniel took the wheel as talk turned to when they would marry. Content in the knowledge neither of them wanted to rush things, Daniel was the first to say what she was also thinking, "You know, we've trusted the Lord with our lives to this point and we'll go on trusting Him with our futures. We both know His timing is best because we've seen it over and over and over again. So let's continue trusting His timing for this major decision."

"My thoughts exactly. Don't think that means I'm not anxious to be your wife. Nothing could be further from the truth. But I also don't want to rush things that shouldn't be rushed. If God leads us to marry next week or to wait until next year, I'm okay with His direction." She squeezed his forearm and nodded her head to emphasize what she'd said. "To be honest, of those two choices, I'd choose next year. Just look at how fast the past twelve months have flown by. You have responsibilities that go beyond a normal job because you answer to a higher power and because you have a whole congregation to look after. Also, I'll not just be taking on a husband but a husband with those responsibilities."

"You mean you'd be okay with waiting a year? I've been thinking the same thing. A year gives me time to continue settling in at church and to do things around my house to get it ready for you." When she laughed, he said, "Don't laugh so hard! I know anyone could walk in and see right off that it's a bachelor's home, but it has possibilities. Right?"

"Of course it does! Your house is great, but there are some things that we can do to make it more of a home for two." Looking at him with a surprised grin, she asked, "Hey, did we just agree a year sounds right? I mean, that's what it sounded like and I'm for it."

"Cayden, a year from today will be a Saturday and would be perfect for a summer wedding! So is that it? One year from today you'll walk down the aisle as Cayden Dewitt and walk back up it as Mrs. Cayden Garrett. Wow!" Stopping the engine, he lifted her off her feet and swung her around. "I love the sound of that—Mrs. Cayden Garrett!

Daniel docked the boat and helped her onto the deck. He would come back out and make sure his boat was properly taken care of, but they wanted to join the family and announce their good news. They knew the family was home by the lights shining brightly in many of the windows. Deciding to make a grand entrance instead of just walking in the back door, they walked around to the front door and rang the doorbell, knowing no one would be expecting it to be them. When his mom answered the door, she was surprised to see who it was but then she seemed to understand there must be some significance to them making an entrance. Her eyes immediately flew to Cayden left hand and she almost screamed when she saw the lovely engagement ring. Daniel held his finger to his lips and she only gasped as she pulled them into the house. About that time, Julie and Grace came into the living room to see who was visiting at this time of night. When they spotted the happy couple, they were not as quiet as their mother in asking questions and figuring the situation out, because Julie squealed while Grace started bawling. Hearing all the commotion, the remaining family members rushed to join them, sure something was wrong, but then got swept up in all the engagement excitement.

An hour later, amid lots of back slapping and congratulations, Daniel dragged Cayden away from his sisters so they could go share the news with her parents and Don and Beth. He tossed the boat keys to his dad, asked him to take care of the boat, and then swept Cayden away. This engagement excitement was fun!

Buddy greeted them at Beth and Don's front door when they silently let themselves in. Cayden quickly picked him up so he wouldn't make more noise, and they followed voices down to the family den. Don and Paul were watching a Braves game while Beth and Meg played a board game, none of them realizing for several seconds that they had company. Don was first to see them when he got up to get a glass of tea and he gave a startled gasp, which caused the others to look their way.

"You could give a guy a heart attack sneaking around like that!" he informed them as they walked into the room. "Buddy didn't even give you away. What gives?"

Eyeing them suspiciously, Meg and Beth walked over with questions in their eyes. Beth was first to speak, "You're home earlier than we expected. Everything okay?" About that time, Meg gave a gasp of her own and came rushing toward Cayden, which made Beth's eyes open wider as she realized what Meg was thinking.

Unable to stand it a second longer, Cayden announced, "We're engaged!" and held out her hand for them to see her beautiful ring. Meg grabbed her first and then Beth while Paul and Don were shaking hands with Daniel. Then Paul was next to grab his girl in a bear hug before letting her go in order for Don to hug her tightly.

After telling them all about their dinner cruise and his romantic proposal, Cayden excused herself to call Allie. When Allie answered, she tried to speak calmly instead of shouting her news. "Hey, Allie, are you still at the movies?" Allie said she and Luke were just leaving the theater and going for ice cream, which gave Cayden an idea. "Would you want to come by the apartment for ice cream sundaes? We've just gotten back from visiting with

Daniel's family at Lake Anna and I've got all the makings for sundaes or banana splits." She could hear Allie checking with Luke and then she came back saying they'd be there in about ten minutes.

Daniel and Cayden hugged everyone again and said their good nights. By the time Allie and Luke arrived, they had everything ready for ice cream. Conversation was lively, with funny excerpts from the movie they'd just seen and plans for tomorrow's church picnic. When they were sitting around the table eating ice cream, Cayden casually drummed the fingers of her left hand on the table waiting for Allie to notice her ring. Ever the elementary school teacher, it didn't take long before Allie reached over to cover Cayden's hand and still her fingers, like she would do with one of her students. Cayden stopped drumming and Allie rejoined the ongoing conversation while Cayden remained still and quiet, watching her friend so that she could see when realization set in. Then, there it was—that sort of confused look, squinting eyes, and rewinding the scene to actually see what was different. And, at last, realization followed by squeals of delight. Cayden jumped up as Allie did and the girls hugged and cried and laughed while chattering and looking at her ring. Luke and Daniel sat in amazement and wonder at what could only be a girl thing. After things calmed down, the two couples enjoyed coffee while Daniel and Cayden told them all about their evening.

Allie suddenly asked, "Have you called Ila yet? I don't remember where they are this weekend, but you've got to tell her. And Marta! What about Marta?"

The rest of the evening was spent making phone calls and then talking about wedding plans. While the girls launched into talk about dresses and flowers, the guys went next door to retrieve Buddy and take him for a short walk before his bedtime. When they returned to the apartment, Luke announced it was time for them to get going and Allie agreed. After bidding them good night, Daniel and Cayden sat quietly for a few minutes enjoying the calm and enjoying the wonder that they were engaged. When Cayden stifled a yawn, Daniel realized it was time for him to go home too.

"I love you, Cayden, and I thank the Lord for you every day. Tomorrow will be a busy day with the picnic and then more family time in the evening. If you're okay with it, we'll start the picnic off with our wonderful news, which by the way, will thrill everybody. Some of them have been dropping obvious hints that it was time I put a ring on your finger before you got away." Although they laughed, he was actually serious. Some of the ladies in his church didn't mind sharing their thoughts about his need for a wife.

She quickly agreed, adding, "This is a big deal for us but also for your congregation because I'll be their preacher's wife. And, Daniel, you have my promise that I'll be the best wife I can be with the Lord's help and grace."

Chapter 12

Cayden and Daniel agreed she would wear her engagement ring on a chain around her neck as she helped set up for the church picnic and then wear it proudly for all to see after the announcement. Promptly at ten, Daniel called everyone together to pray and kick off the festivities. But before he prayed, he happily announced their engagement amid shouts of "Congratulations," "I told you so," and a few "It's about time." The day was off to a wonderful start and got even better when Cayden heard a familiar voice calling her name and turned around to see Ila and Phillip coming her way. The two girls closed the gap between them and hugged each other with tears streaming down their happy faces.

"Ila, you're here!" Cayden almost shouted with glee. "When we talked last night, you were over three hours away and didn't mention coming home today."

She poked Phillip in the ribs before matter-of-factly stating, "I told my sweet husband here that I was coming to this picnic with or without him and he chose to come along so that we could both celebrate your engagement with you." Taking Cayden's left hand in hers, she added, "Now, let's see this magnificent ring!"

Phillip left them to find Daniel and offer congratulations and was almost run over by Allie, who had just arrived and was making a beeline for her best friends. He knew his wife would be caught up in girl talk for quite a while, which meant he had plenty of time to join some of the games being played and grab some home-cooked goodies along the way. He found Daniel, Luke, Allie's brothers, and Brandon playing basketball with some of the other guys and was quickly drafted to play on their team. Church picnics were the best!

Later that afternoon, when the festivities ended and the cleaning up was all done, Cayden and her parents freshened up and joined Daniel and his family for a relaxed meal at the lake house. After such a busy, fun-packed day, everyone was ready to just kick back and enjoy the cooler early evening breezes and casual conversation as they discussed the day's activities. Following a dinner of leftover picnic food, which the kind ladies of Aylett Baptist insisted they take home, talk automatically switched to wedding plans and ideas. The men were happy to listen for a while before deciding to take the boat out on the lake. When they returned, everyone agreed it was time to call it a day—so much excitement was exhausting!

Both families joined the good folks of Aylett Baptist the next morning for Sunday school and worship services. It was Paul and Meg's first visit, and they were impressed with the church God had chosen Daniel to lead. His parents were happy to recognize growth in attendance since their last visit. During Daniel's sermon, tears were on more than a few cheeks as his mother and sisters marveled at the man standing in the pulpit and how he plainly preached the Word with obvious love and devotion to God and to the people who made up the church. God was using Daniel in a mighty way, and they couldn't be happier.

When Cayden had called Marta to share her good news, she learned that Marta and Wade were in Williamsburg celebrating their first anniversary and their last stop would be a day at Kings Dominion. They were planning to stop by and visit with Cayden on their way back home to Joslin, Delaware, but the girls came up with a much better plan. After quickly checking with Daniel, Cayden agreed they would meet Marta and Wade and spend the day at Kings Dominion with them. As it turned out, after having fun with rides and a relaxing lunch, the girls found a cooler spot to chat and discuss wedding plans while the guys rode roller coasters. It was a win-win situation for everyone, and they were sorry when it was time to part ways. Marta and Wade would spend the night nearby, get up early the following morning, and travel home.

On the way home, Cayden voiced what Daniel had been thinking, "So much has happened since God led me here. Of course, the best thing is that you love me and we'll be getting married next summer!"

"Yes, I do love you, but God blessed me mightily to have you love me," he added following her train of thought. "I'm now pastoring a wonderful group of people and loving it. Ila and Phillip are busy full time with the Feed My Sheep ministry and watching it grow."

Cayden jumped back in with, "Luke and Allie finally realized how suited they are for each other. God brought Simon and Coral to Southside, and we've become good friends. Oh, He also led Brandon to your church where he's serving faithfully, along with Gil and Joey."

"And what about Liz and how God used Allie and Rae to lead her to Jesus? Then there's Faith and how she's fit right in at church and also seeing signs of her and Brandon growing closer. Cayden, my girl, God is so good!" Daniel said, giving her a quick kiss before the light turned green. "I'm happy thinking about what the next year has in store for us because we'll be walking through it together."

In mid-September, Allie and Luke pulled off the perfect surprise engagement party. They enlisted his parents to help with the ruse by inviting Cayden and Daniel to a cookout at their house for the Southside single adults Sunday school class. Allie found it a lot of fun working with Luke as they planned the menu, shopped, and decided on a few fun activities for the evening. The more time she spent with him the more she realized just how special he was. Growing up together at church, he had always been just one of the guys. Then they both went away to college and came home different but still the same, which didn't sound possible but was the only way she could describe it. Shaking her head, she focused on what was happening now and found herself smiling at where their relationship seemed to be heading.

"Penny for your thoughts," his familiar voice whispered in her ear. "You were smiling so sweetly, but you seemed miles away. In fact, you didn't hear when I walked around the house calling your name. Want to share?"

Enjoying his nearness, she decided to share where her thoughts had taken her. "I was thinking about you and how I'm happy we're dating." Turning to look up at him, she kissed his cheek and twirled away, knowing he wouldn't resist following her.

When he caught up to her and took her hands in his, he let her in on a little secret, "I'm happy we're dating too, just in case you're wondering." As they walked around the house to the back yard where the party would begin in less than two hours, he added, "I believe God's blessed us with something special."

The engagement party was a huge success, and the surprise worked perfectly. All throughout the evening, Allie and Luke wandered through the large group of their friends hand-in-hand, happy just being together. More than one person commented on what a great couple they were.

They had another surprise the following Wednesday night when Ila showed up for church. After the excitement abated, she explained that she would be home for a few weeks in order to take care of things at home, including annual doctor and dentist appointments. No matter the reason, Allie and Cayden were happy to have her back with them.

"I flew into Richmond Monday evening and stayed at Mom and Dad's until this morning. They've loaned me a car to drive while I'm home, which will make things easier. But one thing I insist on is a girls' night sometime soon. When we came back last month there was hardly time to speak. So I am ready to relax with you two and hear everything that's been going on. I want details, girls!" Ila finished her declaration just as services began, but immediately afterward a plan was made to meet Friday night at her apartment. All three girls had lots to share and they couldn't wait to share it.

After a quick dinner, they settled in Ila's living room with coffee and dessert, ready to talk and talk and talk. Ila started with, "Since y'all pretty much know what's been happening with us through our newsletters and phone calls, I don't have a lot new to share. Phillip is in Dallas for a Bible conference, where he is only one of many preachers getting their batteries recharged. He's not speaking, but that doesn't mean he won't be talking to anyone who'll listen about Feed My Sheep," she said with a grin that made them laugh because they all knew Phillip and his enthusiasm wouldn't be contained. "He'll be passing this way at least twice over the next few weeks, so we won't be apart the whole time. And, of course, we'll talk all the time on the phone and FaceTime, but it's still not the same as actually seeing and being with him."

She and Cayden were surprised when Allie absentmindedly agreed, "Yeah, during the week, Luke and I talk but we see each other only two or three times, depending on what's going on." She finished her statement with a small sigh, seeming to be in her own world for a minute.

So she was surprised when Ila said, "Whoa, whoa, wait a minute here!" and Cayden just looked at her with a knowing smile.

"What? You know Luke and I are dating. Why the surprise?" Allie asked.

"Well, yes, I knew you were dating and I've been happy for you, but what you just said and how you said it tells me it's more than just dating. Cayden, from the look on your face, I think you're thinking the same thing. Right?" Ila kept looking at Allie as Cayden chimed in.

"Oh, Allie, I've seen subtle differences when you and Luke are together, but I agree with Ila. Are things really changing in your relationship, like getting more serious? Come on, girl, give!"

Allie sat up straight and cocked her head to the side like she was deciding how to reply. "Okay, I just re-ran that conversation through my head and I see your point. And, to answer you, Cayden, I do believe things are changing. All the time we spent together planning your party was such fun and we both enjoyed it. I guess you could say we've gone from friends dating to serious dating." Now, her smile was huge and her whole demeanor brightened as she finished with, "And I like it!"

Of course, the conversation continued through dessert and a second cup of coffee. Then, it led to Cayden and wedding plans, which took up the next few hours. When one of them gasped and announced it was past midnight, they decided it was time to call it a night. As they took dishes into the kitchen and loaded the dishwasher, Ila leaned against the counter and shared one last tidbit of information.

"One more thing, girls." When Allie and Cayden turned to look at her, she simply announced, "I'm pregnant!"

Now they were hugging and jumping together as they all talked at once, blending tears with laughter. Ila filled them in on the details. "I took a home pregnancy test that was positive, but Phillip and I agreed I should see my doctor before getting too excited and sharing our joy with everyone. We've only told our parents and asked them to wait until we give them the green light to tell anyone, which I'm sure has been hard. Now that you know, we'll let them know they can tell the world. And before you ask, you're free to share with anyone. I don't want to hold it in any longer. It almost killed me Wednesday night not to shout it to you and everyone at church!" By Sunday, most of the congregation at Southside knew Ila and Phillip's great news. Those who didn't were happy when Pastor Harwell congratulated Ila from the pulpit. There were some exciting, joyful things going on at Southside.

Simon noticed that Coral was quiet when they got home from church, but she said she was just tired. So when she laid down to take a nap, he gave her a kiss and left her alone to rest while he started on the sermon he would preach the following Sunday when Pastor was on vacation. By the time they were ready to go back for evening service, she seemed fine and Simon was glad she felt better.

Monday morning, Coral called her office and let them know she wasn't feeling well and would be staying home. Simon had already gone to the office and didn't realize she had called in sick until he stopped by at lunchtime to pick up some papers he'd accidentally left in his study. He was surprised to find her asleep on the couch with tears still wet on her cheeks. He stood looking at his precious wife trying to decide whether to wake her up in order to find out what was wrong or to let her sleep, when she opened her eyes and, upon seeing him, fresh tears began to fall.

She looked so small and lost, which prompted him to pick her up and sit down cradling her in his lap, rocking back and forth and holding her tightly. He was quiet, waiting for her to calm, until she began to moan, which made him fear she was seriously ill.

"Coral, you're scaring me. Are you okay, honey? What can I do?" he asked, not knowing what else to do. When she clung tighter to him, he did the only thing he knew to do—pray. As he held her and prayed, he could feel her body relax and hear her breathing return to normal. "Sweetheart, do I need to take you to the hospital or should I call the rescue squad? Please tell me what to do."

In a small voice, she began to share her heart. "I'm okay, Simon. Nothing's wrong with me physically. Unless a broken heart is considered a physical problem."

Relieved she wasn't ill, Simon reached to the end table and picked up the tissue box, offering it to her before he tenderly asked her, "Have I done something to break your heart? Or has someone else hurt you?"

"No, you haven't done anything." Getting up from his lap, she walked into the kitchen for a glass of water and returned to sit beside him on the sofa. "When Cayden told me that Ila's pregnant, I was happy for her and Phillip, truly happy. I fought the feelings of sadness and things not being fair Saturday night and Sunday morning. I mean, we've been married over five years and we'll never have our own child. I'll never get to come home and tell you I'm pregnant. Ila's been married for just over a year and is experiencing something I've always wanted to experience."

When she stopped to take another sip of water, Simon spoke gently to his hurting wife. "First, I'm sorry I didn't recognize you were in pain. Next, I understand how you feel because I had a moment, a stab of pain. I always thought we'd have children with your sweet personality, my charm, and your good looks, and that obviously isn't what God has planned for us." Now it was his turn to reach for the tissues to wipe his face.

Coral laid her head on his shoulder. "I'm sorry. I didn't even think you might be struggling. You've been so strong through all our hurt and disappointment that I forget your dreams were dashed too."

Simon was quiet a minute before he turned to look at her and say, "Here's the thing that helps me, Coral. That dream was dashed and it's hard, but God has given us a new dream. When our adoption is approved and we bring the child God gives us into our family and home, we will be their Mommy and Daddy."

"I know, Simon, but it has always been my dream to have a baby." Her tears had stopped and she seemed calm as she simply stated the fact.

Taking her hand again, he shared something he'd only come to grips with himself. "Very early this morning, I spent time on my knees over this very thing and the Lord showed me something. When I really looked at my dream, I realized it was for a child to love and raise—to be a daddy to the child or children God would give me. I still have that dream, but now I know it will come through a different way than I'd always thought." He stopped to see if she was following or if she had anything to say before going on. "Here's what I would like you to consider—not now, but give it some time to really consider and pray about. Has your dream always been to actually give birth to a child or has it been to be a mommy? Will you do that for me, and we'll talk again this evening? I don't want to leave but I need to be at the hospital with Mrs. Abernathy before she has surgery this afternoon. Will you be okay? With Pastor out of town, I should be there, but I can see if Daniel would help out."

Smiling for the first time, Coral reached up and touched his face before letting him know she would be fine and it was all right for him to leave. And she meant it. She was okay and she needed time to think about all they'd said and to pray. Before he left, he held her close and prayed to the One who loved them best.

When he came home later, he found her calm and with dry eyes and dinner was on the table. Over a delicious chicken casserole, Coral shared her heart again after time sitting at Jesus's feet, resting in His love. "I thought about what you said and prayed, asking the Lord to help me think clearly. My dream is to be a mommy. A part of me will probably always be a bit sad to never give birth, but I am happy knowing God is in control and hopefully He will bless us with a child or children in His timing. I also asked for Him to help me be patient as we wait."

She was shocked when Simon jumped up and ran into the living room. When he came back, he was holding a large manilla envelope in his hand.

"Seeing you happy and smelling this wonderful meal got me sidetracked. This was in the mailbox," he said as he handed the envelope to her.

Coral took it and saw the return address—the organization they were working through to adopt a child from China. Taking a deep breath, she took her knife and opened it, withdrawing several sheets of paper. When her hands began to shake, she handed the papers to him saying, "Simon, you read it and tell me what it says. I'm so excited that I can't do it."

She watched as he read through the letter and perused the additional two sheets. As he read, he began to smile and his smile grew as he finished his review. "We've been approved!" he shouted, as he got up and pulled her to her feet in a big hug. "And according to this, there may be a child available in the near future!"

The rest of the evening was given to celebrating and praising the Lord. Simon would contact the organization the following morning as instructed in the letter. He could hear Coral singing in the shower and knew she was okay. As he got ready for bed, he quoted Cayden, "God is good all the time and all the time God is good!"

The next morning while working on his sermon for Sunday, Simon realized God was leading him in a totally different direction than earlier in the week. He took his Bible and slipped into the empty sanctuary, where he sat quietly talking with and listening to his Heavenly Father. As peace enfolded him, he understood the message God would have him share with the people at Southside on Sunday morning.

As Simon had walked past Cayden's desk with his Bible in hand, she knew where he was going. She pretty much knew that anytime she needed to find him, she should look in the sanctuary first, and she always loved it when his time there ended in heartfelt shouts or songs of pure praise. When she heard his rich baritone voice singing "How Great Thou Art," she knew His time with the Lord had been sweet indeed. She added her alto to his melody and joined in the praise. He walked back in the office singing, stopped at her desk to give her a high five as they continued singing, and went into his office finishing the last chorus. Cayden couldn't wait to hear the sermon God had just laid on Simon's heart.

Allie made a point Sunday morning to talk to Coral just to see if what she thought she'd picked up on last week had been her imagination. She had called Coral Wednesday and she seemed fine, but talking face to face could tell so much more. The Coral she found working in the kitchen before Sunday school was a much different Coral than she'd seen last Sunday. She was upbeat and smiling and there was no indication of turmoil, which put Allie's mind at ease. She had been a bit worried that Ila's announcement might make Coral sad, but all seemed to be well.

Simon's sermon wasn't an in-depth study or a long oratory. It was simply a message straight from his heart, which had come straight from God. What he and Coral had experienced over the last few days had led him to the topic and God had provided the text.

After sharing several verses from Psalm 23 and Psalm 37, he prayed and then began sharing what God had laid on his heart. "I had an entirely different sermon just about finished and, to be honest, I thought it was one of my best to date." Laughing, he continued, "But God had a different message for me to share with you today. Actually, you might say it's a second-hand message because He sent it directly to my heart first because He knew I was struggling, and He wanted to remind me of a few things. Then He laid it on my heart to share with you, and I'm glad because I believe we all struggle from time to time with trusting that He has a plan for each of our lives.

"Most of you know that Coral and I have applied to adopt a child from an orphanage in China. But what some of you may not know is that earlier this year we were told we wouldn't be able to have children of our own. You see, our hearts have been broken over this news and I believe we may always grieve for what we know we cannot have. That kind of grief can bring even the most devout Christian to their knees. But the good news is that on my knees was exactly where I am supposed to be when troubles overwhelm me and pain seems almost unbearable.

"Cayden can tell you that I love to come here in the sanctuary when no one is around and just sit quietly and commune with Jesus. What she may not know is that I also come here when I'm at a loss for what to do or my heart is so burdened I can only cry out His name. Don't get me wrong, this sanctuary isn't the key to finding answers or hearing from God. I can do that anywhere at any time, but the quiet solitude seems to be a balm for my weary soul, maybe somewhat like the Garden of Gethsemane was for Jesus.

"I came here Monday morning around four looking for the peace and rest that comes only from God. Like a little child who has skinned his knee or gotten scared of something runs to their dad, I ran to my Heavenly Father and found Him waiting to soothe my soul and guide me. My Good Shepherd led me beside still waters and restored my soul as I poured out my heart to Him and listened to His voice reminding me I am not alone, reminding me He will never leave me or forsake me. He also reminded me that when things don't work out the way I think they should, they will always, always, work out according to His perfect will. You see He has a higher purpose than what I can see or even imagine. I just need to delight myself in Him, stop fretting, trust Him, and wait because even when I don't think God is working, I can rest assured that He is working and He's working on my behalf.

"So in closing I want you to remember this: Even when we don't understand His ways, know that His plan is best and trust Him to fulfill His will in your life. Remember that with Him, timing is more important than time. We see things in relation to how we consider time, but He sees the whole picture and works His plan according to His timetable."

Looking out over the congregation, he smiled and motioned for Coral to join him on the platform. From the look on her face, everyone knew she was surprised but she walked up and took his outstretched hand. With tears streaming down his face, he finished his message. "Monday morning, I couldn't see past the hurt of never having a child. Then God reminded me that if He ever places a child in our family, he or she *will* be my child and I will be his or her daddy. Through God's grace, Coral and I both have come to understand this and trust that God is working things out for our good." By now tears were flowing freely throughout the congregation.

"Then, Monday evening, we received a large manilla envelope. You know, one of those official looking envelopes, which it was because it was from the Christian organization we are working through to adopt a child. Want to know what was inside?" He stopped and smiled down at Coral, who could only smile back. "It was a letter saying we've been approved to adopt and that a child might be ready for adoption before long."

The room erupted in applause and shouts of "Amen!" After just a minute, Simon added, "You see folks? His will and His timing are perfect!"

Chapter 13

Liz had enjoyed her time away over the summer visiting family in Pennsylvania. Although she had texted and called frequently, she was excited to spend time with Rae and Allie and share how God was working in her life. When she called to let them know she was back home, Allie quickly invited her to join the family for dinner that evening. Last year, she would have been terrified at the very thought, but now she jumped at the chance to visit with the whole Lambert family and then hopefully have some quiet time with her two best friends.

Allie's dad Richard met her at the door and welcomed her in as he headed out to the barn for some last-minute chores before dinner. Allie had kept her up to date on how the new farm was working out and if Gil was enjoying his job as manager. From all indications, everything was going well as they worked out a few kinks here and there, and Gil was loving every minute of it. She was sure he would be ready to tell her all about it later, and she hoped Joey would update her on what was new in his life. While she had enjoyed her family, she had still missed this one.

Gil came into the kitchen after washing up and was surprised to find Liz helping his mom get dinner on the table. His surprise grew when she turned around and smiled at him. The somewhat withdrawn, sometimes sullen woman he'd met earlier in the year was gone and a woman with dancing eyes and a bright smile was looking at him sort of quizzically. Then he realized she must have asked him a question when his mom poked him in the side and asked if he had soap in his ears.

"Sorry, Liz, my mind had wandered. What was that again?" He took the bowl of potatoes from her hand and placed it on the table, giving her his full attention.

Laughing, she repeated her question about the farm, and he was all too happy to reply. By the time everyone had gathered at the table, Liz knew a lot more about organic farming than before and she realized she had enjoyed Gil's obvious enthusiasm.

Allie and Liz cleaned up the kitchen before joining Rae in the den. Liz had wanted to share her news at the dinner table but didn't know how to say it. Knowing Jesus was still so new to her. But now she was about to pop if she didn't tell them what had happened just before she left Pennsylvania.

"You know how I told you Grandma taught me about Jesus? Well, she also shared her faith with my mom and dad, but they just pushed it aside as something only old people cared about. But when I told my mom how I had asked Jesus to come into my heart and save me from my sins, she started crying and asked me to explain what that meant. I took out my little Bible and showed her the verses in Romans you shared with me. And she did it! She prayed and asked Jesus to save her too!" Liz finished her story with laughter and tears and heartfelt joy.

When Rae and Allie started to rejoice with her, she held up her hand, laughing harder and saying, "That's not all! When she told my dad, he prayed too. Both my parents know Jesus!"

Shouts of joy and cries of praise filled the room and spilled out into the rest of the house and out through the windows. Richard came to make sure all was well and got pulled into the celebration, which was still going on when Gil and Joey came back in from the barn and they joined in the praise. A year ago, Liz wanted nothing whatsoever to do with Jesus and today she was rejoicing in the fact she loved Him and that her parents loved Him too. Amazing!

When everyone calmed down and the ladies were alone again, Allie suggested something she was pretty sure Liz and her mom would like. "I've been praying about starting a Bible study and inviting the other teachers. It could be here at the farm one night a week and we could do Cythia Heald's *Becoming a Woman of Prayer* study. I was getting ready to start the study by myself and then thought how wonderful it would be to share it with others. It would be a way to fellowship and get to know the other teachers and to share the Gospel with them. Is that something we could do together?"

118

Liz was quick to respond, "I was thinking the same thing! Of course, I didn't have a particular study in mind, but to do something where we can tell them about Jesus would be great. I'm in!"

"Well, you know I would love it!" Rae chimed in. "Which day of the week should be do it? The dining room table would be plenty big for a group of ladies to sit around it and have room to spread out their Bibles and study books." And from there, the plans just rolled out for the first Blessed Acres Ladies Bible Study Group.

Later, as Rae and Richard were about to head up for the night, Richard commended his wife for the godly example she was for their daughter and her friends. "Allie's blessed to have you as not only her Mama but also as a friend and sister-in-Christ." When Rae laid her head on his shoulder and hugged him tightly, he added "And I'm most blessed to have you as my forever sweetheart."

The first Tuesday night their Bible study group met, three ladies from school joined them, along with Aunt Barbara, Cayden, and Faith. It was an introductory meeting where books were handed out and where Allie, as leader, explained how they would proceed. A prayer list was started and prayer lifted up for all on it. By the third week, two additional ladies joined them and the fellowship around God's word was a joy. Of course, after discussing the week's lesson and prayer, they sat around the table enjoying refreshments and getting to know one another. Even some of the women who had worked together for years were getting to really know each other. Liz was finally letting them get to know her and they were amazed at her transformation, which opened doors for her to witness to them. Allie and Rae started back doing something they'd done when Allie was in high school but hadn't picked back up after she returned from college—they prayed together each evening and asked God's blessing on the ladies in their group and especially that He would use them to lead others to know Him as their Savior.

In November, Allie was surprised to run into Luke's old girlfriend Karla at the mall. She had finished shopping and decided to pick up a pretzel as a treat for the ride home when someone tapped her on the shoulder and she turned to see Karla smiling at her.

"Hi, Allie! Seems like old times when we would meet up with friends as teenagers here and couldn't wait to get a pretzel. How've you been?" she asked while perusing the menu.

"I've been well and staying busy. Sometimes it seems teaching is more filling out forms and learning new regulations than actually teaching the children," Allie replied and then thought how dumb that probably sounded. It was a bit awkward talking to someone Luke had dated for a while.

"Luke says the same thing even though he teaches at a Christian school," she shared, before giving the cashier her order. Conversation was cut short when the server handed Allie her order, giving her the perfect opportunity to tell Karla good night and leave the mall.

She couldn't help but think that Karla had moved to Kansas a year ago, but yet she talked about Luke like they were still great friends. Then she realized it was just because this was a recurring theme each year for teachers and Luke surely had mentioned it to Karla many times. But still it seemed odd.

When Luke called that evening, Allie was going to tell him about seeing Karla, but he was in a rush because of parent-teacher meetings and there wasn't time. She decided the grown-up thing to do would be to just forget about it and she did, or she mostly did. This kind of thing was new to her. Anyway, she rationalized, Karla was the past and she lived several states away.

A few days later when Luke picked her up for a double date with Brandon and Faith, Allie had all but filed Karla away out of her mind. She was looking forward to dinner and bowling and hopefully getting to know Brandon and Faith better. Over dinner, there was a lot of smack talk about who was the best bowler and which couple would have the best score by night's end. Allie enjoyed a lot of sports including bowling and loved a challenge, but she and Luke had to admit defeat after two games. Brandon was a good bowler, but what they'd heard about Faith was true—she was a great bowler. On the way home, Allie and Luke decided a lot of their dates would be spent improving their bowling scores, especially if they were going to ask for a rematch someday.

The week of Thanksgiving was always fun for Allie for several reasons. Anticipation was almost palpable, not just among the children but in everyone. Cooler temperatures meant digging out warm sweaters, toasty fires in the fireplace, pumpkins and scarecrows on the porch, and hot cider or cocoa in the evenings. Of course, a three-day work week contributed to her joy, along with the promise of family around the table enjoying a delicious meal and thanking God for His bounty and watchcare throughout yet another year. She was looking forward to this Thanksgiving even more than usual because Luke would join her family for their mid-day meal, and she would join his for their evening meal. They really were an actual, bona fide couple and she was happy.

Monday after work, she ran into Fredericksburg to do some grocery shopping and pick up some things at Hobby Lobby. After finishing her errands and eating a quick fast food dinner, she decided it would be nice to stop by the academy and see if Luke had finished working with the basketball team, stopping at a coffee shop nearby to pick up a cup of his favorite peppermint mocha. As she was pulling away from the drive-thru window, she glimpsed someone who looked like Luke at a table. When she looked again, she saw it was Luke and that Karla was seated across the table from him. Startled, she quickly drove on around the building and into a parking space. She sat there for a couple of minutes trying to decide whether she should go inside and act surprised or just go home. In the end, she decided to leave the coffee in Luke's car and went home. Her heart told her there was a perfectly good explanation for what she'd seen, but her mind told her heart that might not be true.

She was glad no one was in the kitchen when she came in and put the groceries away. So many questions wove themselves through her mind. Why was Karla still here and not back in Kansas? Had Luke's practice time been cancelled? Why were they there together? Was there any significance to them being together? The final question was if she believed Luke would do anything to hurt her, to which she answered that Luke wouldn't purposely do something to hurt anyone and especially not her.

As she put the last item away, her mom walked in the kitchen to put a cup in the sink. Happy to see her daughter home safe and sound, she asked when Allie would be ready for their prayer time. When Allie didn't reply immediately, Rae stopped rinsing her cup and looked up to see Allie silently wiping tears from her face.

"What's wrong, child? Has something happened? Are you hurt?" she asked as she gently folded her sweet girl in her arms.

Regaining her composure, Allie put her mom's fears to rest, assuring her she was fine. "I need to shower and get ready for bed. Could we do our prayer time in my room instead of at the kitchen table? Maybe meet me there in half an hour?"

Rae agreed and Allie went upstairs. She would meet Allie in her room for their prayer time, but she promptly sat down at the kitchen table and petitioned the Father to help with whatever was on Allie's heart. Allie wasn't prone to easy tears, so Rae knew whatever was wrong must be major. When the grandfather clock chimed the hour, Rae knocked on Allie's door, ready to listen and help if she could.

After Allie told Rae what she'd seen, Rae was as confused as Allie, and she agreed Luke wasn't the sort of man to purposely hurt her. "So you left the coffee in his car?" When Allie nodded agreement, she continued, "You know some girls would have 'accidentally' spilled it on the driver's seat." This caught Allie unaware and made her chuckle, which was music to Rae's ears.

"Would you pray with me, Mom? Then I think I'll give him a call. I can't go to sleep wondering what's going on." Mother and daughter, two sisters-in-Christ, bowed their heads and prayed for wisdom and guidance and for sweet comfort regardless of how Allie's talk with Luke went. Just as they finished praying, Allie's phone rang, and Rae excused herself after planting a kiss on her daughter's forehead.

When Allie answered, Luke sounded no different than usual. He asked how her day had gone and then asked if she had put the coffee in his car.

"That was so sweet, but why didn't you come in the coffee shop? I'm sure Karla would have liked to see you and you know I would have." Luke didn't seem to see there might be a bit of a problem with the particular scenario he's just described, but Allie did and she was quick to help him see it from her vantage point.

"Luke, do you not get how it must have looked to anyone, but to me especially, to see you sitting with your old girlfriend chatting merrily over coffee? And, besides, what's she doing here? Didn't she move to Kansas?"

"Whoa, Allie! What did you think was going on?"

"Well, I could only think what I saw—you and Karla having a lovely time together." Her voice remained calm, but the sad, confused Allie had been replaced with a woman who wanted answers and wasn't getting them. "I thought it would be nice to stop by the academy to surprise my boyfriend and bring him a cup of coffee, but I'm the one who got surprised."

"I'm so sorry if all this upset you, but it shouldn't. Karla decided life in Kansas wasn't what she'd imagined and she moved back here. The academy is looking for someone to finish the school year for Mrs. Eldridge, one of the fifth-grade teachers who is having a baby and won't be back until next school year. Karla came in for an interview and the timing worked so that she walked out the office door just as I left the gym. I was as surprised as you were to see her, and she offered to buy me a cup of coffee to catch me up on what's been going on. I never gave a thought how it might look or how you might react to the situation."

"Oh," was all she could think to say.

"Sweetheart, Karla and I are still friends, but that's it. Even if she gets the teaching job our paths won't cross that often. Allie, I hope you know I would never ever do anything that might hurt you. You do, right?"

"Yes, I do. I kept reminding myself of that all the way home. Did Karla tell you she and I ran into each other at the mall the other day?"

"No, but we really only talked about the school. I mean, I did ask about her family and why she's back home but nothing more. And then I told her I needed to get home and we left. If it makes you feel any better, I didn't even walk her to her car."

"Well, that's not like you to not walk a girl to her car."

"To be totally honest, it was because she was going to have another cup of coffee and make some phone calls. But if I had walked her to her car, I would not have opened the door for her. How's that?"

When Allie laughed, they both knew the tempest had subsided and all was well. This dating thing was fun and romantic, but it was also hard because no two people thought the same, especially when one was a female and the other a male. After he promised to pick her up after school the next day and take her bowling, they said good night. As she was just about asleep, one thing niggled at the fringes of her memory . . . Luke had called her "sweetheart!"

Chapter 14

The Lambert family enjoyed a very traditional Thanksgiving, with Liz and her parents as special guests. After hearing their big news, Rae had gotten their phone number from Liz and called to introduce herself and invite them to join her family for the holiday. It was the first time they had visited Liz in Virginia, and she was ecstatic to show them her home and what she now considered her town. After dinner, Rae and Richard gave them a tour of the farm ending with Rae's little goats.

Cayden spent the long weekend with her family in Virginia Beach while Daniel, who as a pastor was always on call, enjoyed Thanksgiving Day with his parents in DC before returning home that evening. Cayden's Grandma Phyllis was happy to have her home for more than just a short visit so that they might have some time together, just the two of them. Since the cold she'd had in August, she hadn't felt totally back to full strength and she felt her age more than ever before. Of course, she jokingly blamed it on the colder weather in Virginia, but she felt something akin to urgency to share with her grandchildren things about her life and about their mother's early years— things that she'd meant to share before but always put off until later. She didn't dare tell Meg or anyone how she was feeling for fear it would distress them, but for her it was a relief, something like ticking an item off a to-do list. Carter, who was in his first semester at Old Dominion University, sweetly sat and talked with her when he came home for visits and she tried to keep the conversations light and not too long. But Cayden was about to experience one of the great joys of life when she married her sweetheart in less than a year, and Phyllis wanted to impart whatever wisdom she could to aid her as she transitioned into her new role as a wife who would also be taking on the great responsibility of pastor's wife.

As it happened, Meg and Paul both had to work the Friday after Thanksgiving and Carter was busy with Clarissa, which left Cayden and Grandma Phyllis to enjoy a whole day together. It was a joy for both women to talk about everything under the sun as they worked on a large jigsaw puzzle together. When Meg returned home that afternoon and joined them, she was happy to see her mother looking more like her old self with a bit more pep in her step. As Cayden drove home Sunday afternoon, she thought about many of the things Grandma had shared with her and felt joy in knowing she had such a heritage of godly women supporting her.

After Thanksgiving, Christmas preparations at both Southside and Aylett Baptist kicked into high gear, keeping everyone busy. A combined Christmas party for single adults from both churches was held at Mr. Dean's home with a huge turnout. Mrs. Dean let Daniel know she would take care of everything so that he and Cayden could enjoy their last singles Christmas party. The highlight of the evening was the gift exchange that was quite unusual and loads of fun, with Liz winning the title of Miss Christmas Elf. At the end of the evening, Mr. Dean read the account of Jesus's birth from Matthew Chapter 1, which brought back childhood memories to many of them of their fathers reading the story to the family on Christmas or Christmas Eve. Everyone agreed it had been one of the best Christmas parties ever.

Christmas break from school seemed to fly by way too quickly, and Allie felt like she hadn't spent much time with her friends. So the Sunday after Christmas she declared they must have one of their visits to Olaf's after service that evening. Since Daniel's evening service started earlier than Southside's, the contingent from Aylett Baptist arrived at the restaurant first and procured tables to seat a dozen people. When the others arrived and they had all ordered their food, they set about filling each other in on how their holidays had been and what was going on in their lives.

Surprisingly, Liz was the first to speak. "I've had the most wonderful Christmas and all because for the first time I actually celebrated the birth of Jesus. Sure, there was shopping and decorating and baking and all that good stuff, but underlying it all was the excitement of knowing Him and praising Him and thanking Him." As she spoke, her voice rose in intensity and her fervor thrilled the hearts of her friends. "And what made it all the sweeter was that my mom and dad were feeling the same way!"

Allie piped up next, "My Christmas was extra special, and you, Liz, are one of the reasons why. Your enthusiasm and obvious love for the Lord have reminded me to always be excited about Him too." Giving Luke's hand a squeeze, she continued, "Then there's this fella to my right who I was happy to share Christmas with this year—him and his family. Who knew Jeff and Teresa were so cool?"

"Well, I did, for one," Luke chimed in laughing and then added, "Celebrating with Allie and her family was really special. I'd never celebrated Christmas on a working farm before, but they invited me and my parents over for Christmas Eve and after a huge meal, we did a sort of Bethlehem walk—you know, like they do at some of the churches around here. There were sheep, cows, goats, a donkey, and, of course, a manger. Although I imagine the Lambert's barn is a bit nicer than the stable where Jesus was born, it really gave me a good perspective."

"So you enjoyed the barn animals and that's what made your Christmas special. What about me?" Allie teased.

"Well, of course, that goes without saying. Our first Christmas as a couple has been wonderful, the best Christmas ever. There, how's that? Not too over the top?" he asked with a wink.

"Nope, that sounds just right!" she said while turning to her brothers. "What about you two? Anything special about your Christmas, like maybe the gifts your sweet, kind sister gave you? Hmmm?"

Joey rolled his eyes at Gil before answering, "I was going to chime in if you ever quit talking and tell them about the gift you gave me. Allie bought me one of the tools I've been wanting for the woodworking shop I've set up in one of the barns at Blessed Acres II. In fact, everyone gave me things on my wish list for the shop and that's all I've been doing since Christmas, getting it set up."

Gil added his two cents worth at this point, "Little brother, I won't be surprised to walk in the barn one day and find a bed set up so you can spend all your spare time there." After Joey thanked his brother for such a great idea, Gil continued, "This Christmas has been extra special for me too. I am loving my job at the farm, learning new things every day and trusting myself to do things I've never done before. Dad and Uncle James are teaching me so much and the coolest part is that we're all having fun together most of the time. There are those times of aggravation or uncertainty, but those are just part of farming and animal husbandry. Back to Allie's question—my dear little sister tracked down a set of books on organic farming that I have been borrowing from the library because I was too cheap to buy them myself." And, of course, this brought about much laughter because they all knew Gil's determination to squeeze everything he could out of a dollar. "But what really made Christmas special this year is mostly thanks to you, Pastor Dan."

Chuckling at Gil's use of the name the teens called him, Daniel asked Gil what he meant. "While I'm happy to hear it, what have I done?"

Glad he asked, Gil continued, "I grew up at Southside and love Pastor Harwell, but the decision to join you at Aylett Baptist was the best thing I've done. Daniel, brother, your preaching is amazing, and the Wednesday night in-depth studies are something I look forward to each week. This past year I've grown more in the Lord than ever, and I'm in the Word, not because I have to be but because I want to be."

Realizing how quiet the group had become and thinking maybe he'd said too much, Gil grew quiet, but Joey picked up where he left off. "Yeah, I agree with Gil. I wouldn't trade the feeling of peace and I guess it's joy that I have since I've begun really getting to know Jesus better. And we get an extra dose of it since Allie started the ladies' Bible study. She and mom are always discussing their lessons at dinner and us guys join in. Unbelievable!"

"Uncle James says Aunt Barbara talks with him about what she's learning too," Gil added. "It used to seem odd to walk into the barn and hear Dad and Uncle James talking about things like abiding in Jesus and getting to really know Him. Now, I just join in and we talk as we work."

Liz was wiping tears from her eyes as she glanced over at Allie, who was in full-blown meltdown listening to her two brothers talking so openly about Jesus and their feelings. When they decided to start the weekly Bible study, it was to benefit some of the ladies at school, and she knew she was growing with each lesson. Who knew it would also impact the guys? God, of course!

Always one to find humor in a situation, Joey told them about a special gift their mom had given each man in the family. "Y'all will enjoy this. Mom bought all us guys a copy of the study book, *Becoming a Woman of Prayer*, for Christmas!" Amid their laughter, he added, "But she was kind and marked through 'Woman' and wrote 'Man' in black magic marker." More laughing ensued as Allie came around the table to give her brothers hugs. She couldn't wait to share this with her mom!

Coral laid a photo in the center of the table and, when she had everyone's attention, shared some wonderful news, "This, ladies and gentlemen, is what made our Christmas more than wonderful. Meet the little boy we're going to adopt next summer!" And there went the tears and laughter amid joy again, with everyone offering congratulations and hugs to the proud parents-to-be.

"We'd been given a heads up to expect the photo and information sheets. So when it came the day before Christmas Eve, we decided to wait and open the envelope on Christmas morning. Of course, we fell in love with him immediately and then read through the paperwork describing him and his physical problems. The orphanage has given him the name Bo, which we're told isn't pronounced the way we would say it but it means 'abundant.' We like that and plan to leave that as his name. Bo is three years old and has been diagnosed with high-functioning autism. But look at his bright, shining eyes and that big grin. You can just see his happy, bubbly personality," Simon finished with a grin to match Bo's. The hope of one day holding their little boy in their arms and loving him had brought pure, uncontainable joy to his prospective parents.

"And one more thing," Coral added enthusiastically, "In addition to Bo coming to us in the next few months, we've also been approved as foster parents, which means we could get a call to care for a child at any time. So I will happily be giving my two weeks' notice at work next week!"

After everyone finished sharing about their Christmas, Daniel led them in a brief prayer of thanksgiving and praise before they went their separate ways. Just listening to the excitement about what God was doing in their lives made them look forward to what was to come in the new year, and they all agreed that, no matter what, they could rest assured God was in control.

Chapter 15

*I*n January 2020, Southside celebrated the second anniversary of their Feed My Sheep ministry under the dedicated and enthusiastic leadership of Ellen's husband Connor. The ministry had grown, and volunteers were blessed as they worked to help others. Their biggest challenge in the winter months was to find shelter for those who wished it and to check on those who declined a warm bed for whatever reason. Connor's network of local churches and benevolent organizations was often stretched to the limit in order to lend aid and encourage those in need.

Since the ministry began, there had been several who had made a profession of faith and some who had accepted assistance in reconnecting with their family or friends. Two of the men who had accepted Christ were now members of Southside and a great help in the ministry. Through the ministry, one woman had reached out to her family for the first time in five years and had been reunited with her children just before Christmas. Every success was celebrated with praise and thanksgiving, but then they all got back to work in order to prepare for the upcoming weekend services and meals.

On a trip home in early February, Phillip was happy to chat with Connor and hear how well things were going. He and Ila would be in town for a few days before traveling to Mississippi for meetings at several churches. Afterward, Ila would come home and travel with Phillip only to nearby meetings until the baby was born in early April.

He met with Pastor Harwell and Daniel the day before leaving for Mississippi to catch up on their ministries when talk turned to the outbreak of pneumonia in China. The pneumonia of unknown cause had been named COVID-19, and more than 1,000 deaths had already been attributed to it.

"On the news this morning, they reported at least 15 known cases in the United States," Pastor Harwell advised. "There have been cases in other countries, also. Simon, Cayden, and I are contacting our missionaries by either texting or emailing to see how they're doing."

Daniel nodded in agreement and suggested something he'd wanted to pass by these two seasoned preachers. "I've been contacting our missionaries too, and Eric Brevton in Thailand has a couple in hospital with what they are now diagnosing as this COVID-19. On another note, John, one of the men in my congregation, is a safety officer for George's Electric, and I've been talking to him about giving a brief update to our congregation, along with things to do during flu season to help mitigate spreading any type of virus. Do you think that would be adding to fears or helping?"

Pastor Harwell and Phillip agreed it would be beneficial, and Pastor jotted down John's contact information so he could talk with him as well. Before they went their separate ways, Phillip led them in prayer for guidance in this troublesome time, for healing for those with the virus, and especially for God's protection for His missionaries around the world. As they walked out to their cars, Daniel put into words what they were each feeling. "I believe this thing is going to get a lot worse and not just overseas."

Meanwhile, wedding plans were in full swing since August was only six months away. Cayden and Allie took a quick trip to Virginia Beach to spend the day with Cayden's mom and Grandma Phyllis and discuss some of the details. Although Grandma still wasn't back to her normal perky self since the summer cold that knocked her for a loop, she was doing pretty well and was happy to be a part of planning her granddaughter's wedding.

First, Cayden shared her list of bridal attendants, which held no surprises: Allie and Marta, maids of honor; Ila, matron of honor; and Carter's girlfriend Clarissa, bridesmaid. Daniel had chosen Luke as best man and Phillip, Simon, and Carter as groomsmen. From there, they drafted lists for flowers, music, colors, etc., before jumping into ideas for the reception. By the time Allie and Cayden started home late that afternoon, they were happy but exhausted. Although it was lots of fun, this wedding stuff could take it out of you!

Ila and Phillip were in Mississippi celebrating Valentine's Day, which was also the second anniversary of the day Phillip proposed. The day was special but rather low-key since the trip down had tired Ila out, which only confirmed their decision that this would be her last long trip until their baby arrived. They had made the decision to not learn the baby's gender until he or she was born. However, at Ila's last check-up, they finally gave in to their curiosity and asked the doctor to write it down and seal it in an envelope, which they would open on Valentine's Day. So after dinner and several chocolate truffles, they opened the envelope and learned that soon they would be holding little Wyatt Lee Doucet in their arms.

Back home, Southside's Sweetheart Banquet was quite the social event at the Spartan Inn, which Cayden and Allie considered quite swanky. Everyone jumped at the chance to dress up a bit and shake off the winter blues for the evening, especially Allie and Luke. Since it was their first Valentine's Day as a dating couple, they enjoyed the occasion to put on their finest and dine in style, and they were not alone. After a sumptuous four-course meal and music by none other than Joey and his friends, Luke drove Allie home the long way just to prolong their lovely evening. The more time they spent together, the more he knew for certain he was in love with her. He just needed to figure out when to share that information with Allie.

Chapter 16

*I*n late February, the first person died from COVID-19 in the United States, and the country was briefed to brace for what might come. Phillip left for two meetings in Florida on March 10, flying out of Richmond. Allie had volunteered to stay with Ila while he was away. Even though Ila would enjoy the company, she didn't think it was necessary since baby Wyatt wasn't due to make his appearance for several weeks. But she gave in so that Phillip wouldn't worry about her the whole time he was away.

Allie had taken the day off and offered to take Ila shopping for some last-minute baby things. After taking Phillip to the airport, the girls shopped 'til they dropped, which didn't take long since Ila gave out pretty quickly. As she napped, Allie worked on lesson plans for the next day. It was nearing the end of the school year and there were a lot of things to cover before turning her second graders over to a third-grade teacher. The school year had been quiet, especially compared to the previous year with all the drama over weekly religious education classes, but she still looked forward to summer and spending time with Luke. He had mentioned his parents were talking about a trip to Scotland and wondered if she'd like to go with them, which thrilled her. She'd never left the United States and Scotland was definitely on her bucket list. Before she knew it, she had her laptop open searching major sights to see and what the weather would be like in June or July. Daydreams of castles and rugged landscapes kept her occupied until Ila woke from her nap announcing she was hungry.

Luke had spent his day teaching history to students who had early symptoms of spring fever. During his free period, he spent time in the school library searching databases for information on historical instances of anything similar to what was currently going on in the world. He'd spent some time over the weekend talking with Daniel, who shared what he was learning from conversations with missionaries in countries already affected by this new strain of pneumonia that was responsible for many deaths in a very short period of time. Daniel's level of concern had ramped up his own, which meant it was time to see what he might learn from the past. As Solomon said in the book of Ecclesiastes, there was no new thing under the sun and that included a mysterious virus that might bring great devastation not only in China but also in his own country.

While Cayden was daydreaming of her wedding and looking forward to trying on her wedding dress the next day, Daniel was considering how he could help missionaries on the front line of the COVID-19 problem. He also found himself wondering if someday soon he might be dealing with the same problems, which prompted him to ask his audiovisual gurus to meet with him that evening.

Over subs and pizza at his house, Daniel explained what he was learning from talking to missionaries, especially Jake Fauntleroy in Rome. Italy was a hot spot for the virus and was restricting gatherings, including church services. Jake's main need was prayer, of course, but next was the need for audiovisual equipment that would enable him to share services online. Faith was quick to remind Daniel that they still had the old system they'd recently updated, which prompted them to discuss if that equipment could help Jake. The final decision was to get it shipped to him the following day.

The next discussion wasn't quite as easy because it revolved around how they would proceed if faced with the same problems. Gil summed it all up when he shook his head and said, "While I'm praying our country won't face what others are, the bottom line is we can pray but we should also prepare. After all, anything we learn concerning what our new system is capable of will come in handy later."

Brandon, whose interest in audiovisual equipment had been sparked by his work at church, was taking night courses at the local community college. He thought for a minute and then agreed. "This has been discussed at school since we first heard about the havoc this virus is causing in China, and we've concentrated on software, programs, and Internet sources for ways to share information and meet when in-person meetings aren't possible. The church's new system will be invaluable if we need it to broadcast using some Internet platform like YouTube or even Facebook."

Daniel felt more at ease as they closed their very productive meeting with prayer. They had come up with a preliminary plan, a plan they hoped to never need.

The next day, March 11, two major things happened. First, the World Health Organization declared a COVID-19 pandemic. There were more than 118,000 cases in 114 countries, and this unknown pneumonia had already claimed over 4,200 lives. Many people in the United States had never heard the word *pandemic* and, if they had, it certainly hadn't pertained to them and their families. Slowly but surely, it began to sink in that a crisis was at hand, and no one was sure if the world was prepared for what was looming just ahead.

Second, but of no less importance to Allie, Ila started having contractions, which she insisted were only Braxton Hicks contractions. Baby Wyatt wasn't due for another two weeks and she wasn't concerned and, therefore, saw no need to tell Phillip. He was already working on a way to get home since the earlier pandemic announcement and would be back in plenty of time.

Allie wasn't worried. Since Ila was a nurse, Allie trusted she knew what was what and listened when Ila told her to go on to school. However, when she got back to the apartment after work, worry kicked in big time. Ila was pacing around the living room with her hand on her lower back and a pinched look on her face.

Without thinking, Allie quickly asked, "Ila, are you okay? Are Braxton Hicks contractions supposed to make you look like you're in really bad pain?" Her last word was lost when Ila let out a long, loud moan. By the time Allie got to her, she was sure that Ila was in real labor.

Catching her breath, Ila gave a brief but succinct update. "My water broke just before you arrived, and my contractions are coming fast. Grab my bag and get me to the hospital." She finished this with tears of frustration because only a few minutes ago she'd realized Phillip would not be at his son's birth.

Things moved fast from that point. Ila had called her doctor, who was also a close friend, and she was waiting for them as Allie pulled up to the emergency entrance. The doctor didn't want Ila to spend time in emergency since the waiting room was full of patients with flu and possibly COVID. She handed Allie a mask to wear and a note that would allow her to come up to the obstetrics ward after parking her car.

As she walked into the hospital's main entrance, her phone rang. Seeing it was Phillip, she sat down near the elevators and smiled, hoping the smile would be reflected in her voice because she wasn't really smiling inside. After bringing him up to date and assuring him Ila was in the best hands, Allie asked about his plans for getting home.

"Flights are impossible, and everyone is trying to find rental cars. So I contacted the pastor here who has insisted I take his car. He's on his way over to the hotel now and I'll be leaving shortly after he arrives." His voice was husky as he added, "Allie, please take care of her for me. I won't get there to see my son born."

Allie felt like he'd punched her in the stomach and tried to think of something to say that could possibly help. "Phillip, I promise to do everything I can to take care of Ila and baby Wyatt." Wiping away tears, she suddenly had a thought that might work. "If the doctor will allow me to be with Ila, I could Facetime with you so that you can be there. Would that work?"

The first thing Allie heard was a shout and then, "Allie, that would be perfect! I'll call as soon as I'm on the road. But once the doctor says it's okay, call and I'll pull over and park so I can be there one hundred percent. Thank you so much, Allie! Give Ila a hug for me and tell her I'm praying."

The doctor agreed with Allie's plan and even had one of her nurses take care of the call when the time came so that Allie could focus on helping Ila. In what seemed like no time at all, Allie was instructed on gowning up and what to expect next. They connected with Phillip, who pulled off the interstate, found a safe parking area, and began coaching his wife. Seeing his face and hearing his voice seemed to give Ila extra strength and visible peace.

Allie had seen lots of farm animals give birth and was always amazed, but nothing prepared her for being in the delivery room with her long-time friend. Listening to Phillip offer sweet encouragement to his wife was precious and seeing how Ila, who was always so strong, let her guard down and allowed him to share her pain was almost too personal to watch. Then things started moving really fast and within minutes, Ila and Phillip saw the face of their son, who was letting everyone know he was in the house.

Phillip arrived at the hospital the next day in plenty of time to take his wife and son home. The doctor might have kept them in a day longer but felt comfortable discharging them in light of the current health crisis. Allie had gone back to the apartment to make sure all was ready for little Wyatt and to pick up her suitcase. Cayden met her there with food offerings from Beth and Ellen and flowers from her and Daniel. They were just about to leave when the happy family walked through the door and Ila introduced Cayden to her son. Cayden asked to hold the baby and Allie was next in line, which meant they didn't leave for another hour. Wyatt's hair was as dark as his mom's and his eyes were the same shade of blue. But everyone agreed the dimples in his cheeks were identical to his dad's. Both sets of grandparents were expected to arrive the next morning and had rooms reserved at Ellen's Shamrock Inn, which was good because yet another change was on the way.

Chapter 17

$\mathcal{T}$he next day the President of the United States declared a nationwide emergency and travel bans, which was soon followed by the state shutting everything down. Hospitals closed their doors to visitors and most public schools suspended classes for the remainder of the academic year. Many businesses began to scramble to find a way to go forward without employees coming in to the office or establishment. Human Resources and Information Technology Departments worked around the clock to put plans in place so that employees could work from home in order to keep businesses open while keeping everyone as safe as possible.

Allie and Liz were part of the task force at their school assigned with collecting each student's personal belongings and packaging them so that their parents could stop by the school and pick them up over the next two weeks. Other teachers took on the task of giving the packages to parents when they pulled up to the school during specified times. Masks were worn and social distancing of at least six feet was followed, which added to the strange atmosphere that prevailed at the school and everywhere.

It was surreal to walk down the empty hallways knowing their students were sequestered in their homes and they wouldn't see them again for the rest of the school year. Allie had written a note for each child in her class and slipped it in with their things, along with books she'd bought as end-of-year gifts at the winter book fair. As she worked, she prayed for each of the children and their families.

Luke had a different two weeks after the country was shut down. Because the academy where he taught was a private school, those in charge decided to follow CDC guidelines and outfit classrooms and common areas so that social distancing rules were followed and children would miss only two weeks of classroom instruction. During the first week, teachers scrambled to use the academy's student portal in order to provide lessons and instructions until children were welcomed back. In between making sure his class lessons were ready to post each day and answering student and parent emails, he helped with the necessary renovations to ready the school for the children's return.

Each evening, he called Allie, and they gave each other much needed encouragement. When a good teacher is faced with situations where they're sure their students will be challenged, they are determined to help in any way possible, and Luke was a very good teacher. This meant that at the end of each day he was mentally and physically drained during those first two weeks.

Although the children were a bit tentative at first, they were happy to be back with their friends even if it meant wearing masks, keeping their distance from each other, and other new rules. However, after a few days, the prescribed guidelines were the new norm and things began to settle down as time passed.

Daniel found himself very busy. He met with his deacons and the decision was made to suspend all services and activities and to immediately do what was necessary to livestream one service on Sunday morning and one on Wednesday night. Brandon had worked hard to set up a YouTube channel for the church, with Faith and Gil helping him work out all the kinks in order to be ready when it was needed. For the first services, Daniel would lead in one hymn with Cayden playing piano and then he would preach. This would keep the number of people coming into the church to a minimum. After each service, a volunteer crew would come in and deep clean the sanctuary in hopes to keep down any chance of spreading the virus.

Cayden helped by sending out letters, emails, and texts to everyone who attended Aylett Baptist so they knew how Daniel was handling the situation and how to access the livestream sermons. Thanks to thinking and planning ahead, Daniel's people missed only one Sunday without being able to watch services that, while different, were still something familiar and uplifting and something they all needed.

The second week after the country went into lockdown, an elderly couple in Daniel's church fell ill and were admitted to the ICU. He felt helpless as he sat in his car outside the hospital each morning praying for them because no visitors were allowed, not even their children. It hit hard when their son called to say both his parents had passed away during the night and Daniel couldn't even be with him to offer a shoulder to cry on or quietly lend support.

During his time as pastor, he had performed only one funeral and now he was going to preach a double graveside service for two people he held dear. He was having to feel his way along in order to follow state guidelines as well as how to help the family.

Cayden could see the huge burden he was carrying along with the daily matters he still attended to, and her concern began to grow. He was trying to do anything and everything possible to help others, and it was beginning to wear on him physically and emotionally. When she came to dinner at his house that evening, her heart broke for this man who loved so freely and deeply and gave of himself so tirelessly. This prompted a conversation that would shape their lives going forward.

After supper, which he hardly touched, Cayden decided to share her heart with him. "Honey, I wish there was some way I could help with the burdens you're bearing." When he only looked at her with sad eyes and a weak smile, her resolve was strengthened to say what she felt God had laid on her heart. "From the get-go, we agreed a big wedding wasn't something either of us really wanted, and we agreed to wait until August to get married. However, that was before a pandemic hit our world and everything changed. I believe we should regroup and set a new date for our wedding."

"Are you saying we should postpone our wedding past August?" he asked looking even more sad than before.

"No. I'm saying we should move the date up to sometime next week," she quickly assured him.

At her words, Daniel put his head in his hands and wept. He cried for what was happening all around them, for those who were ill, and for those who were grieving. And he cried because Cayden had just said what his heart wanted to say. Moving closer to him and directing his head onto her shoulder, she cried along with him.

When their tears subsided, Daniel lifted his head and shared his heart. "For the last two days, I've tried to think of a way to tell you that I can't do this alone, that I need you by my side now. But I didn't want to deprive you of the wedding you've been dreaming of and planning for."

Cayden took his face in her hands and gently kissed him before speaking. "I only want a wedding. If it's only you, me, a justice of the peace, and two witnesses, so be it. I want to be your wife and helpmate. So I checked and, believe it or not, the county has set up a drive-thru for things like getting a marriage license. We fill out the necessary paperwork, go there, pay the fee, and we're in business. So the question, my love, is how soon do we do this? Just so you know, I'm ready to marry you tomorrow."

All melancholy gone, Daniel became a man of action. They reviewed online what was needed and how to go about it, printed out the forms, and made plans to go to the county offices the next morning. He picked her up so that they would arrive when the office opened and drove away with a marriage license in hand. Over breakfast at her apartment, they made plans for how to get married in just two days. Date and time set, they contacted four people who would be very important to the success of their wedding plans.

The wedding would be held at Aylett Baptist and Pastor Harwell was more than happy to officiate. Luke and Allie were thrilled to be their witnesses and Brandon would take care of videoing the livestream, which would be open for everyone to view. While it broke their parents' hearts to not attend the wedding, they were happy to be a part of it, although from a distance.

Two days later, Daniel and Cayden pledged their hearts and lives to each other and began their new life together as husband and wife. Their joy was evident even to family and friends watching via livestream. They had met three years earlier in circumstances where Cayden had chosen to follow God's leading. Over time, they had become friends and had fallen in love. Now they were ready to face the future together, still following His lead.

When they arrived at their home after the wedding, they found a wonderful surprise. Using a key Daniel had given Beth for emergencies, she and Ellen had secretly set up a delicious brunch for the newlyweds. While not what Cayden and her mom had been planning for a reception, it was perfect in every way, including fresh flowers on the table and wedding gifts from several friends. There was also a small but beautiful wedding cake, complete with a topper that looked a lot like the bride and groom, which they would enjoy later that day.

Who knew honeymooning during a pandemic with travel restrictions could be such fun? Both of them had taken three days off to celebrate, hopefully relax, and forget about what was happening around them. Buddy was enjoying time with Don and Beth, and they would pick him up in a few days when they would also begin moving Cayden's things to their house.

Living on a small lake with access to a larger lake offered so many possibilities. They took the boat out on Lake Caroline in the early mornings, sometimes for a leisurely ride around the lake and a little fishing and other times to feel the wind on their faces as they skimmed along the water. Evening walks around the lake took a while but were filled with getting to know each other better as they walked hand-in-hand, sharing stories from their childhoods and memories of family vacations. Spirited tennis matches were really fun because they both loved to win and usually the winner was absolved from cooking dinner, adding to the level of competitiveness.

After the honeymoon, Cayden pretty much worked from home, where she had set up an office in one of the bedrooms. Daniel already had a room set up as his study and used it often but mainly still went to the church to work, wanting to make sure his people knew he was accessible. As they returned to the real world, they were glad and encouraged to face it together.

The pandemic was about as real as it could get, and the end was nowhere in sight. By mid-April, more than 18,000 people had died from COVID in the United States, and confirmed cases had hit the half-million mark. Hospitals were pushed beyond their limits. Due to the pandemic, some businesses closed temporarily and others shut their doors permanently, resulting in unemployment at an all-time high. Groceries and supplies of everyday items such as paper towels and toilet paper were often hard to come by. In just one month, the world had changed and the virus raged on, resulting in more devastation and hurt.

Chapter 18

*I*n late April, Luke came home from the academy feeling tired and battling a headache. Believing stress to be the culprit, he took two Tylenol and laid down before even thinking about fixing something for supper. His mom called a couple of hours later just to chat and see how his day had gone, but after several rings she was redirected to voicemail. She left a message and finished cleaning up the kitchen, but all the while fear niggled at the back of her brain. When she called again with the same result, she decided to call Allie.

After the usual pleasantries, she asked, "Allie, have you talked to Luke this evening? I've called twice since school let out but he isn't answering."

"I was about to call you and ask the same question. He usually calls me after he gets home and changes clothes, but he didn't today. So I've been calling too." Allie had been a little concerned but now she felt sure something was wrong. Grabbing her purse and keys, she headed out the door. "I'm getting in the car and going over to his house. Can you get there quicker?"

"Yes, we're leaving right now. We'll meet you there," Teresa almost shouted as she ran out the door, all the while explaining to Jeff what was going on. When they saw Luke's car in the driveway and no lights on in his townhouse, they knocked once but then used their emergency key to let themselves in. They found Luke on the sofa sleeping. When Jeff turned on the lights, Teresa gasped.

"Jeff, he's soaked!" Feeling his forehead, she added, "And no wonder! He's burning up!"

Jeff tried to wake him, but he only moaned quietly. "We've got to get him to the hospital. Help me get him up and to the car. It'll be faster than waiting for the rescue squad."

Allie arrived just as they were leaving, and Jeff motioned for her to follow them. The hospital was less than five minutes away, but it seemed like an eternity before they pulled up to the emergency entrance. Jeff explained the situation to the door attendant and soon Luke was moved onto a stretcher and taken inside. Safety protocols would not allow any of them to accompany Luke, and their hearts broke as they watched as he was taken away from them.

Fearing that Luke had COVID, Jeff and Teresa would not let Allie hug them or touch them. As they clung to each other crying and praying for their only child, Allie leaned against the wall and dissolved into tears. When she felt strong arms enfold her, she looked up into her father's face. When they had all regained control, Teresa filled Allie and Richard in on the little they knew.

The hospital attendant walked them through the process for filling in online forms, which Teresa promptly took care of, and then he gave them a paper with Luke's case number and instructions for obtaining information. Not being able to be with Luke was tearing them apart, but they just had to wait and pray.

When the attendant walked away, Richard didn't even ask, he just started praying aloud. "Father, we know you have this under control, that you're holding Luke safely in your arms. Please guide the doctors and nurses to find out what's wrong and give them the ability to treat it. You know we all love him but more importantly we know you love him. Give Jeff, Teresa, and Allie comfort and a calm spirit as they wait. Lord, you are the Great Physician, please heal Luke. As always, we pray your will be done, but we ask again for his healing. We ask this in Jesus's name. Amen."

Tears still flowed but a much calmer spirit prevailed. They discussed the possibility of taking shifts in the parking lot waiting to learn what was happening, but none of them could leave. Richard announced he was going home and would bring back coffee and some blankets and probably his wife. He felt better when that last bit made Allie smile faintly.

He returned an hour later with Rae and the things she'd pulled together that they might need for what would probably be an overnight stay in their cars. Richard noticed as she was putting stuff in his truck that she'd brought along items he recognized were for her. Mama bear wasn't going to leave baby bear alone, and he wasn't surprised. In fact, he wasn't so sure Papa bear was leaving either.

Rae had also called Cayden, who let Pastor Harwell know and activated the prayer chains for both Southside and Aylett Baptist. She and Daniel then drove quickly to the hospital armed with more supplies that might be needed. On the way there, she texted her parents and Daniel's parents and sisters asking for prayer.

When they pulled into the hospital parking lot, they easily found Allie, Jeff, and Teresa, who were surrounded at a safe distance by others from church. As they were asking Jeff if there had been an update yet, his phone rang. The ringing phone stilled everyone in the group. The conversation was short and Teresa couldn't read Jeff's face to determine what was being said, but she could tell it wasn't dire news or maybe she just hoped it wasn't.

"That was a nurse. Luke tested positive for COVID, and his case is severe enough to warrant putting him in the ICU." Jeff's voice broke after making such a statement about his son. "He is being given the very best of care, but that was all she was able to tell me for now." Reaching for his wife, he held her tightly as they wept together for their boy.

Daniel's hand tightened around Cayden's, causing her to look up at him where she saw pain and she understood what he must be thinking. The last time he heard this same pronouncement he was sitting in this same parking lot and within twenty-four hours his two sweet friends were dead. Now he was hearing it about his best friend. Bowing her head, she prayed not only for Luke but also for her husband.

This time, it was Pastor Harwell who led them in prayer. When he finished, he gently suggested that Jeff and Teresa might want to go home and get some rest, to which, he was quickly and kindly told, they weren't budging, at least for now. But Jeff extended the suggestion to everyone else. It was approaching midnight. Daniel began singing "Great Is Thy Faithfulness" and soon the air was filled with the lovely words proclaiming God's mercy and love. Within a few minutes most had left, with promises to continue in prayer for one of their own.

A car pulled up beside Cayden and Allie and Ila rolled down her window. "We weren't going to come, but I just had to make sure you're okay, Allie. What happened?"

Allie filled her in on everything that had transpired since Teresa had called her earlier and finished up with the nurse's update. The nurse in Ila came to the forefront and she asked, "Has anyone alerted the academy that one of their teachers has COVID? They need to know first to pray but also to put their remediation plan into action. Allie, when was the last time you were around Luke?"

"Three days ago when we had dinner at his house. Why is that important?" She asked before realization dawned on her. "Oh, no. Does that mean that even though I've not seen any symptoms, I might pass it on to others?"

"From what I've read, yes. The incubation period is two to fourteen days, which means you might want to quarantine yourself for a while. And, please, please be aware of signs of any of the symptoms so you can be treated quickly. Promise me you'll do that, okay?" Ila was speaking as her friend but also as a nurse.

Allie promised but then began to think of who she'd been around since that time; it was just those on the farm. She was immediately glad she had maintained social distancing with everyone else, even when she would have loved to cry on Cayden's shoulder earlier. Thanking Ila and Phillip for coming and promising to send updates, she went in search of her family.

As expected, Teresa and Jeff and Allie and her parents spent the night in their cars. Leaving was just too hard, and sleep wasn't coming no matter where they might be. Around four, the nurse called again just to say there was no change and was quick to add that no change meant Luke was no worse, which was a good sign. Again, she encouraged them to go home and get some rest, but they couldn't.

That evening, Cayden received news that Grandma Phyllis was ill. Carter called just as soon as their parents left to take Grandma to the urgent care center. He tried to be brave, but Cayden could tell he was shaken. She and Daniel discussed what to do and decided she should join her family in Virginia Beach in case she could be of any help. As she was packing, her mother called to say Grandma did have COVID and told her not to come. In fact, her actual words were, "Under no circumstances are you to come." Cayden might have considered going anyhow, but her mother's message was too emphatic to ignore. She didn't want Cayden walking into a quarantined house.

Cayden had talked to Grandma Phyllis the afternoon after her wedding and knew she still sounded weak. Her strength had not fully returned since she was sick the previous summer. But she was so happy to have been a part of Cayden and Daniel's wedding, even if it was only via livestream. Now Cayden was praying for this woman who meant so much to her and who had always been a role model of a woman who loved God and served Him with her whole heart.

Three hours later, Cayden's dad called letting them know Grandma Phyllis was with the Lord. Her last words had been, "Lord, I'm coming home." After which, she smiled and closed her eyes.

Cayden's heart was heavy for her mother, and she wished she could be with her but knew it wasn't possible. She would see her family in three days when she and Daniel went down for the graveside service, which Daniel was honored to lead, but it wouldn't be the same because her mom, dad, and Carter were officially in quarantine. They would be keeping a distance from anyone attending the service. The song "In the Sweet By and By" kept playing in her head, a gentle reminder that she and Grandma would one day sing together again with no pain or sorrow, with only praise for their Lord.

In the meantime, Allie was continuing her vigil in the hospital parking lot and taking time to go home only to shower, grab a quick nap, and return. Teresa and Jeff took turns and found solace in Allie being there. They kept their distance but spent time each day talking. She learned things about Luke's parents she'd not known, and some of it helped her see how much he was like both his mom and his dad. On the second morning, the nurse's update added to their anxiety. Luke had developed difficulty breathing during the night and the doctors were trying one of the new drugs that had been developed to successfully fight COVID. The nurse promised to call back in a couple of hours, because it took the new medicine time to start working and for them to see a difference.

Cayden came by the hospital to check on Allie and, to be honest, draw strength from her best friend. Allie had a way of making her feel like things were going to be all right, and she needed that big time. But when she arrived, it was obvious her friend needed her even more. Keeping their distance, the girls pulled out camp chairs they kept in their cars, sat down, and just talked. Each shared news and what was on their hearts and prayed together for everyone and everything. As they talked, they visibly relaxed and conversation drifted to more mundane, normal things—just the thing they both needed.

"So how's married life?" Allie asked. "I don't know if I told you, but your wedding was the most romantic wedding I've ever attended."

Cayden looked to see if Allie was being funny but realized she was serious. "Really? For me, it was extremely special, but as weddings go, there was nothing to make it stand out. What made it romantic?"

"The couple getting married. The unusual circumstances. The reasons they moved their wedding date up. Sort of like watching an old black and white movie during wartime when the couple realizes they want nothing more in life than to be married to each other and live and face life together no matter what happens." She stopped to get them sodas from a cooler in her car and returned to see Cayden smiling at her while crying buckets of tears. "Oh, sweetie, did I say something wrong?"

"Nope. What you said just touched me so much because that's a great picture of our wedding and our reasons for changing the date. The tears are because I truly cannot even begin to imagine how I would be handling everything right now without Daniel with me, and I believe he feels the same way. Luke being so ill has all of us feeling so helpless but not hopeless because, Allie, I really believe God will heal him. Then Grandma dying is hard because I'll miss her so much, but I know she was more than ready to meet the Lord since she's been sick for months. What might be hardest is not being able to be with Mom, Dad, and Carter, but they will not allow me to come near them just in case they might be contagious. Speaking of which, it's killing me not to hug you, my friend, for you but also for me. I don't think you know how much you sort of ground all of us." Cayden stopped to sip her drink and allow Allie to speak, because she could tell her friend had something to say.

"This not hugging thing is really hard, Cayden! Thankfully, since I'm quarantining with my family, we hug each other, but my first inclination when you called about your Grandma was to jump in my car and come to you. Since none of us is showing any symptoms, we just have a few more days to quarantine and then I'll be hugging everybody, probably even the mail carrier." Hearing Cayden laugh was just what Allie had hoped would happen. But she certainly meant what she'd said—social distancing and being in quarantine were not fun. "Oh, and thanks for saying such a nice thing about me!"

Teresa and Jeff had brought over their chairs and joined them, making a large circle. Luckily, it was pretty quiet, and they could hear each other even six or eight feet apart. As they were offering condolences to Cayden, Jeff's phone rang, and they sat on the edge of their chairs waiting to hear what news was coming. This time, Teresa could definitely read her husband's face because he was beaming and grinning from ear to ear.

When he ended the call, he turned to them and shouted, "He's reacting to the meds and fully awake. His breathing is getting better hourly and he said he's hungry!"

Teresa couldn't speak but Allie could. "Praise the Lord! Are they keeping him in the ICU? Is his fever down?"

"She said they are thinking they may be able to move him out of the ICU tomorrow morning if he has a good night. His temperature is only slightly elevated, and they're thinking this medication should help with that also." Jeff was so happy he started running around their circle. "My boy's getting better! Thank you, Jesus!"

Cayden left them to share the news and to update the two prayer chains. This was too big not to share immediately. Luke was on the mend!

One week after Luke was admitted to the hospital, he was finally discharged and taken to his parents' home. COVID had taken a huge bite out of his physical stamina, and it was taking a while for his clarity of mind to improve. However, once he was home under his mom's care, each day showed big improvements. Allie and his parents were happy that their quarantines were over and none of them had gotten ill, because that meant they could spend time with Luke. Allie visited for just a little while each day, as much for herself as for him, because she needed to be near him after the stress of not knowing what was going to happen.

With great joy, Luke walked back into his townhouse after a week of his mom's tender care. Thanks to Allie and Teresa, his refrigerator was full of things he liked, and his house was clean from top to bottom. The academy had closed after he had fallen ill, and a thorough cleaning was done before students were allowed back three days later. He would be off one more week before returning to work, which was good because just moving back into his home had worn him out. The week would give him time to build endurance and be ready to teach again, just in time for school to close for the summer.

Chapter 19

Since the beginning of the COVID crisis, which had originated in China, Coral and Simon had been concerned about the orphanage where Bo lived and the health of all the children and workers. At first, they received two short messages confirming that the orphanage wasn't experiencing problems, mainly because they pretty much lived in isolation already. But they hadn't heard a thing since the third week in March. As the pandemic grew and the entire world was affected, their common sense told them that the chances of bringing Bo home to the United States in 2020 were pretty low, but they continued praying. To them, Bo was already their son. So while they cared and prayed for everything going on in their own country, their hearts also hurt for Bo and the other children and workers in the orphanage.

While so much was going wrong around them, Brandon and Faith were growing closer and enjoying time together. Faith and her aunt were now working full time from home, as was Brandon. So they felt comfortable to think of themselves as a family unit of sorts, meaning they could freely visit without having to practice social distancing. As the pandemic worsened, this was a blessing in many ways since they felt comfortable sharing meals and helping each other out, but mostly having others to share everyday life with. It was also good for Faith and Brandon as they worked the audiovisual equipment together at church, a ministry they were growing to enjoy more and more.

And then there was the added blessing of being able to get to know each other better. During such troubled times, added pressures often brought out parts of a person's personality they didn't always allow others to see, and that had some advantages as a couple grew together. They could see the good, the bad, and sometimes the ugly before long-term commitments might be made. It was like sharing a bathroom with a roommate for the first time and realizing they had some habits you didn't care for, but you learn to accept them and go on. Then when it's time to renew your lease, you decide if those habits are dealbreakers. You've seen the good, the bad, and the ugly and can make an informed decision.

One thing they particularly liked was their time studying the Bible together. When the pandemic hit, Faith's Aunt Georgia had just started a new study of the book of Hebrews with the ladies at church. Since they were no longer meeting, she asked Faith if she would like to do the study with her, and Brandon asked if he could join them. So each Tuesday evening, the ladies either came to his house or Brandon went to theirs for dinner followed by Bible study together.

Georgia commented one evening, "You know, since we really socialize these days only with each other, our time studying after the evening meal seems like what it must have been like in the old days before the advent of cars." When she saw the odd looks Faith and Brandon were giving her, she laughed and finished her explanation. "Without the ability to travel here and there easily, families were their own company. They didn't have the distraction of television, the mall, or cell phones and some didn't even have a lot of books. But most families did have a Bible and they would have actually had time to spend together reading it and possibly studying together like we're doing."

"I hadn't thought of it that way, but I agree. Maybe one night we should do our study by oil lamp or candles," Brandon said jokingly.

But Faith obviously didn't think his idea was funny at all. "I love your take on this, Aunt Georgia, and I even love your idea, Brandon. Let's plan to do that next Tuesday night."

Georgia detected the excitement in Faith's voice and was happy to agree. "We'll have a *Little House on the Prairie* dinner and study time. Brandon, don't look so scared. You'll love it. After all, it was your idea," she said with a wink.

The ladies hadn't had so much fun since COVID hit. Georgia remembered some dresses she had packed away from when she had volunteered as a docent at a nearby historic farm, and they enjoyed first finding the boxes in the attic and then rummaging through them. A few alterations were needed but when Brandon arrived Tuesday night, he found two pioneer women busily getting dinner on the table. At the end of the evening, he declared that was the best dinner theater he'd ever attended, which earned him kisses on his cheeks from his hostesses. Faith treasured all these wonderful times in her heart as she grew more in love with this special man God had put into her life, and Brandon wondered how long he should wait before asking Faith to marry him.

Allie was so happy that Luke was back at work and regaining his strength. She was staying busy preparing for what she hoped would be a new, normal school year at the end of August. However, with COVID continuing to claim lives and disrupt life as they'd known it, her hopes were dimming as the days passed. On the news that morning, she'd heard that now, at the end of May, more than a 100,000 people had died in the United States and there were nearly two million confirmed cases. Her heart ached for the people suffering from the virus and the families of those who had died. But she was most thankful that Luke was better and that so far none of her family had gotten ill. Living on a farm helped since everyone except Joey could just stay on their property and interact with very few other people. Her parents, Uncle James and Aunt Barbara, and Gil worked on the farm and without students to teach, she had little reason to venture out. The contractor Joey worked for was keeping him busy even though supplies were getting harder to obtain. But a building contractor can take on small jobs in order to keep his employees busy and continue to keep his business afloat.

After experiencing firsthand what the COVID virus did to his body, Luke was determined to keep Allie and his parents safe. Other than going to work, where precautionary measures were taken, he kept pretty much to himself. He would breathe easier when the school semester ended. Until then, he and Allie mainly talked each day on the phone. When they did meet, he insisted on observing social distancing guidelines. Although they couldn't play one of Allie's favorite sports, basketball, they were both getting really good at tennis and pickleball.

Luke particularly loved going to the farm for walks and sometimes fishing in one of their ponds. On one of those occasions, as they sat on the bank quietly enjoying each other's company and waiting for a fish to bite, Luke asked Allie something he'd been wanting to know for a while. "Allie, do you think something has changed in our relationship? Do you feel it too?"

She thought for just a minute before replying, "If I'm honest, I believe all my relationships have changed since this terrible pandemic began. So much of what I've taken for granted all my life is different in one way or another. I mean, whoever would have thought we'd be hoarding toilet paper?" They laughed together, lightening the mood a bit.

"But to answer your question, yes, I feel it too. It's almost as if we've grown up since you were so sick. I lived in abject fear that you would die, and facing that possible reality was too much at times to bear. But each time I hit a low spot, God sent someone along with just the right words to pull me back up out of that horrible pit of despair. More importantly, He comforted me in the hours I spent alone in my car praying. I was in the middle of a new Bible study our ladies' group is doing over the phone on Tuesday and Thursday mornings, and each lesson reminded me to trust Him and to remember He has a plan for you. Did that mean I could rest assured you would get well? No. It meant that, no matter what, you were His child and He was caring for you. Even if it meant that His plan was to take you home to be with Him, you would be okay and I would be too because I'm His child and one day I'll be going home to Him also." Allie's face was wet with tears but almost glowing as she finished this last part.

Luke had seen her growing in the Lord over the last year, and her testimony was proof of her love for God and her faith that He would always carry her through no matter what the trial. With a husky voice, he thanked her yet again for how she had been so faithful to pray for him and to uplift his parents. "Mom said there were times when you and she were sitting alone in the parking lot that she felt like her world was crashing around her and you lifted her up. In fact, she told me about the day you two were singing and rejoicing so loudly that others began to look at you like you might have gone over the edge."

Allie laughed with him as she remembered that time. She and Teresa had really bonded during that week, and they even had gotten several chances to share the gospel with others who were also waiting on news of loved ones.

"But back to the original question, we both feel our relationship is different. But do you see it as a good different? Because I do." Luke waited for her answer, hoping they were on the same page here.

"Oh, yes," she replied quickly. "It's like we were in a fun stage before and that was great. Now we're in a new stage and I'm not sure how to describe it, but I like it." The last was said with a perky grin, which set Luke's mind at rest. For now, they would enjoy this new stage and see where it would take them. But he was pretty sure where it would go, and he was happy just being with her.

Liz had decided when schools closed to go back to Pennsylvania for a while. Her parents were happy to have her, and she was glad to spend time with this new mom and dad who loved the Lord. They spent time reading the

Bible, asking questions, and getting to know Jesus better. In early June, she returned to Virginia ready to participate in a committee tasked with devising a plan for online teaching methods for the county students. While she was glad to help, her heart was saddened to face the fact that at least for the immediate future, she wouldn't be teaching her students in person.

She waited a while before letting anyone know she was back home. Although she hadn't been around anyone with COVID symptoms, she wanted to be sure she was clear. As soon as she let Allie know, Allie insisted she come to the farm that evening for supper. Since Liz lived alone, Rae suggested and the whole family agreed that Liz consider herself part of the Lambert family, which thrilled her heart to realize she was loved and accepted by these awesome people.

Even though they all had been more or less staying around home, everyone had things to share with Liz, and Rae enjoyed watching her three children vying for attention. Joy was written on each of their faces as they played catch up on what had been going on in their lives. Allie had been in constant contact with Liz while she was away but still had things to say to this woman who had become more like a sister over the past year.

Liz went to the farm often and helped them with whatever chores needed doing. Allie taught her their routine, and she enjoyed working alongside them. Joey had taken great pride in showing her improvements he'd made to his woodworking shop and promised to teach her how to make a keepsake box like the one he'd made his mom for Mother's Day. She jokingly told him it was a relief not to see a bed set up in the corner.

One morning, Gil taught her how to drive a tractor and rode over with her to Blessed Acres II. On the way there, he pointed out changes they'd made or were in the process of making. It was obvious by the way he answered her questions that he was truly in his element. She noticed the farmhouse wasn't occupied and asked what their plans were for it.

Happy she was interested, Gil answered, "Well, it may eventually be a bunkhouse of sorts since we'll need more help as time goes by and we clear more land to farm. But for now, I have my office set up in one room and you'll not be surprised to know that while Joey may not have a bed set up in the workshop, he does have one in the house. Most days after work he comes straight here and gets lost in his own happy world. Mom has to call and remind him to come home for dinner. Occasionally, he'll be in the middle of working on a special order for someone, and Allie or I will bring dinner over to him."

Liz loved the way Gil talked about his little brother, and anyone could tell he was very proud of Joey and his special gift. "All you Lambert kids have such special talents."

This surprised Gil because he never thought of himself as having any talents and he could feel himself blush. To hide his embarrassment, he said the first thing that came to mind, "I don't have any special talents beyond being the most handsome son with a winning personality."

Liz chuckled and punched his arm as he helped her down off the tractor. "Well, we won't debate that right now, but you must know what your special talents are. Of you three kids, you do have the most outgoing personality, never meeting a stranger, making people laugh, and—most importantly—putting them at ease. But then you inherited a love for farming from your dad, along with the intelligence and curiosity to not just make it work but to excel. You also inherited a calm, assured spirit from your mom."

As they rode back to the house so she could help with lunch preparations, Gil thought about what she'd said and realized it made him happy that she saw him that way. But then conversation returned to normal everyday things like how her work on the school committee was going and what the weather was going to be over the weekend. Having Liz around the farm was a nice thing.

Chapter 20

Daniel was happy how well livestreaming services was working. Cayden and Faith had even worked out a roster for those who would like to provide special music. They would come in to the sanctuary and Faith would video them singing or playing an instrument. Cayden was happy to accompany anyone on the piano. Then Faith and Brandon would work the special into the livestream broadcast. Mostly, Cayden was the only audience as Daniel preached on Sunday mornings and Wednesday nights. Sometimes, Liz or Gil or Joey popped in and sat at the back of the auditorium. He was happily surprised to learn that several people sat in the church parking lot listening to the broadcast on their car radio or watching it on their laptop or tablet. Mr. Dean did this each Sunday morning. When Daniel asked why, Mr. Dean said it was hard to stay away from church, but also that he wanted to be closer by as he held Daniel up in prayer while he preached. Daniel could only praise and thank the Lord and for blessing him with such a stalwart, dedicated servant to work alongside him as he ministered.

When the academy school year ended in early June, the whole staff felt like they could finally relax. The administrator ordered them all to go home and stay away until their first planning meeting in early August. They had done an excellent job both as educators and as counsellors to children who had faced so much over the last few months. Luke drew the first truly relaxed breath he'd taken in months and thanked God for seeing them through what he hoped was the worst of the pandemic.

Two days later, Allie called with devastating news. Joey had died from COVID.

While a farm runs on a schedule, some things are more relaxed than others. Since Joey wasn't part of the actual farming business, he often kept to his own schedule, especially when he had orders to complete. No one minded, especially Rae, because she was thrilled to see her son so happy. Sure, she sometimes got aggravated when she had to remind him two, three, or sometimes four times to come home for a meal, but that was short lived and life rolled along. He was always good about letting her know when he planned to spend the night at Blessed Acres II, which meant she could sleep well not worrying where he was. He continued to play his guitar or violin with his friends and assured her they pretty much kept their distance from each other. At work, he and the guys he worked with were mainly outside, and social distancing usually wasn't a problem with the jobs they were working. So Rae didn't worry about him, or at least not much.

One evening, he missed dinner but called and said he had some things in a mini-fridge in his shop he could put together for a meal. Later, he called again to say he was bushed and would just stay the night there. His usual routine in such instances was to come home early the next morning, shower, grab breakfast, and leave for work.

The following morning Allie left early to meet Liz for tennis and Rae went to the stock yard with Richard. She left a plate with Joey's breakfast on the table with a note telling him she hoped he had a wonderful day and that she loved him. Allie was back first and noticed the plate still on the table. She called him but he didn't answer, which wasn't unusual when he was working. He might not hear it ringing above the noise of power tools or he might be busy. However, as she went into her bathroom to shower, it occurred to her that while Joey might not have had time to stop by for something to eat, he would surely have come in to shower and get fresh clothes. Still not worried but just a little curious, she went upstairs. His bedroom and bathroom doors were open. When she went into the bathroom and opened the shower door, it was obvious from the dry walls and floor that Joey hadn't showered, either. Now she did begin to worry a bit. So she called him again but still got no answer.

As she was coming back downstairs, Gil walked in the back door. Seeing Allie's puzzled look, he asked what was wrong. She ticked off on her fingers what was causing her concern—the uneaten food, a dry shower, Joey not answering her calls. Trying to calm her a little, Gil assured her everything was fine, but inside he agreed with his sister that something was wrong. They both knew it.

Gil started for the door, "Come on, we'll go up to his shop and check. He's been working on a new order and has probably decided to take the day off to work on it. With his machinery running, he wouldn't hear the phone." It all sounded feasible, but still the gnawing in his stomach wasn't abating. Allie took a minute to leave a note for her parents before quickly following him to his truck.

When they got to the shop and saw his truck there, they sighed in unison. Allie was first to speak as they got out of Gil's truck. "He probably let mom know his plans and I've blown this all out of proportion. Sorry, Gil!"

As they approached the shop, they heard no sounds of machinery, hammering, or their brother humming or singing as he always did while he worked. When Gil opened the door and found the shop dark and empty, he picked up his pace as he headed for the house. Allie was right behind him as he took the stairs two at a time, but he still beat her to Joey's room where he stopped in his tracks so quickly she almost ran into him. Then he was all motion as he took two long strides and fell on his knees next to the bed where Joey was gasping for air. He sat on the bed next to Joey and propped him up against his shoulder, hoping that would help his brother get air to his lungs and all the while crooning to him that it would be okay and to just try and breathe.

Allie joined him and through tears asked what she should do. Gil told her to call 911 and then to get some cold cloths to try and get Joey's temperature down. From all indications, Joey didn't know they were with him but they both continued talking as calmly as their racing hearts allowed, encouraging their brother to breathe and telling him how much they loved him. When they heard sirens, Allie ran outside to direct the paramedics to Joey. Aunt Barbara and Uncle James arrived just before the rescue squad. They'd stopped by the house and found Allie's quickly scribbled note telling her parents to come to Blessed Acres II immediately. Aunt Barbara stayed outside with Allie to send the paramedics in as Uncle James went to see how he could help.

The paramedics went into immediate action and asked the family to wait downstairs while they worked to help Joey breath. Tommy Bates, who had grown up with Gil and Joey, was heartbroken to see his friend in what appeared to be the last stage of COVID. He'd seen it over and over, but he always hoped for a better result each time. As they prepared to move Joey downstairs on a stretcher, silence filled the room that had just been filled with the horrible sound of someone who could not get enough air into their lungs.

163

Tommy looked at his partner and they silently shook their heads while checking Joey's vital signs and finding no pulse. His friend's struggle had ended. Now he had to tell the family, something that never got easier especially when they were people he loved.

They all looked up as Tommy walked downstairs alone, apparently in no rush, and they immediately knew. Their brother was dead.

Gil and Allie had been trying to reach their mom or dad, who had obviously silenced their phones or left them in the car because each call went straight to voicemail. A calm washed over Gil as his mind cleared and he knew what they needed to do. He grabbed Allie's hand and pulled her behind him to his truck so they could find their parents and tell them what had happened. The stock yard was only a few miles away, but it seemed to take an eternity to get there. When they pulled in beside their mom's car, Allie found herself wishing she was anywhere in the world but here, the place where her mom and dad would learn their child had died.

They walked through the small crowd looking for their mom and dad, hoping they hadn't left yet. When Allie saw her mom, she touched Gil's arm and pointed to where her parents were standing. They walked slowly hand-in-hand toward the two people they loved most in the world with hearts as heavy as cinderblocks.

When Rae spotted Gil and Allie walking toward them, she waved and smiled like usual. But Allie knew the instant her mother recognized something was wrong because her face fell and she started running to them with their dad following behind wondering what had gotten into her. Gil led them out of the crowd and to their vehicles before telling them what had happened. Rae screamed while Richard stood staring and wide eyed. Then Rae took control and ordered Gil to drive them to wherever Joey was. She needed to see her son.

A quick call to Uncle James and Gil knew to drive to the hospital. When they arrived, he asked everyone to wait until he talked to the attendant and found out if they could see Joey. After a hasty call, the attendant told Gil to drive around to the entrance where he would see the rescue squad still waiting. The attendant there would let them in.

Rae insisted that she and Richard go in first, and her children listened even though they wanted to be there to support their parents and to grieve with them. Later, Rae would explain that first she and Richard needed to come to grips that their family had just changed forever before they could comfort their remaining children as they should. After a few moments, the attendant motioned Allie and Gil to follow him inside, where they joined their mom and dad around their brother. When they came back out a short time later, Richard indicated they should follow him to a picnic table across the road. They sat down, quiet and slightly bewildered. Then he spoke in a strong but broken voice.

"When we get home, even with this pandemic going on, I'm sure there will be people waiting for us. This will be the last time we have together, just us four, for a while. So I think it's good to take a minute to think about Joey and who he was." He stumbled when he had to use the past tense but carried on, "I'll start. He was my baby boy, the one who looked and acted more like his mom than me, which endeared him even more to me every time I saw her when I looked at him, especially when he smiled. He was just as happy holding a hammer as he was holding a violin and he was talented using either of them. Joey was quiet and unassuming but strong and sure of himself, and I was extra proud of him for that. He knew what he wanted and how to get it. This past year or so I've watched him grow in his walk with the Lord and enjoyed it when we all discussed you girls' Bible study lessons at the dinner table. Gil, he looked up to you as his big brother and imitated you in some ways. Allie, he always wanted to protect you, but he also absorbed strength from you. The three of you, each so different yet so alike, made our family circle complete. Now it's not changed because he will always be with us in our hearts, and one day we'll sing together in heaven while he plays maybe a harp—yeah, I think it'll be a harp." He stopped abruptly, evidently saying everything he could say.

Each of them did as Richard had done, sharing who Joey had been to them. When they were talked out, Richard stood up, gathered them to him, and prayed and then they followed him back to the truck. They were as ready as they would ever be to carry on with one of them missing.

While waiting at the hospital to join their parents, Allie had called Luke and Gil called Daniel. When they reached the farm, several cars were in the driveway. Uncle James, Aunt Barbara, and Liz stood on the back porch, while Pastor Harwell, Daniel, Cayden, and Luke stood by their cars. James had apologized for not inviting everyone in and relayed Richard and Rae's insistence the family remain quarantined for the time being. Pastor Harwell waited for Richard and Rae to join the others on the porch before moving to stand in the yard near the porch steps. He would respect their wishes but couldn't leave without speaking and praying with them.

Without saying a word, Liz joined Gil and Allie, who had started walking toward the barn with the others following at a safe distance. Right then was not the time for words but for quiet, like the man they were mourning so deeply.

Joey's death set off a shockwave in both churches. He had grown up attending Southside and was a very active member at Aylett Baptist. He was known, respected, and loved and would be missed by everyone. Rae and Richard chose to have Joey's funeral in the field behind the big barn, setting up like Joey had done for the celebration the previous summer. Afterward, his body was laid to rest in the Lambert cemetery located on the farm. Daniel and Pastor Harwell spoke, sharing memories of Joey and how he loved the Lord, which led to explaining how anyone could know and love Jesus. Family and friends walked behind the hearse to the grave site, accompanied by Joey's buddies playing music he had loved.

After the service, Gil and Allie sat with their parents on the back porch enjoying the quiet and the cool breeze as they discussed the day and eventually the next day. As always, there were things on a farm that couldn't wait, and they were rather glad to slip back into a routine that had always been comfortable and would, hopefully, seem normal. Richard had to pick up the new cows he'd bought at the stock yard, Gil needed to catch up on bookwork, Rae listed chores she should take care of, and Allie would do what she did best—make sure they were all okay or at least as okay as they could be.

The next morning over breakfast, Richard asked Allie to ride to the stock yard with him. When she just shook her head, he decided to speak what was weighing on his heart. "Honey, you haven't left the farm since Joey died. It'll do you good to take a ride with me instead of sitting around here." He'd wanted to say "moping around here" but decided that might sound too harsh. They had another week of quarantine and he didn't want to see any of them, especially his sunshine girl, using it as an excuse to hide away from the world.

Still sitting quietly, looking at her half-eaten breakfast, Allie responded, "I don't even like the idea of venturing out. Nothing's the same and a change in location won't make a difference."

"I know it feels that way, but we can't turn the farm into a bunker of sorts, a place to burrow in and pull away from life. Your mom says you won't let Luke come to the farm even to just go for a walk like you two did after he got out of the hospital. Don't you want to see him or Cayden or Ila?"

"There's a part of me that wants to see them so badly it hurts but another part that doesn't want to take any chance they might get sick the way Joey did." Wiping tears from her eyes, she looked up at her dad. "Luke calls each morning and asks to come over, but I just feel too tired in my spirit to say yes. For right now, talking on the phone works well."

If her tears hadn't been his undoing, her words were enough to make him stand up, gently take her by the hand, pull her to her feet, and tell her to be ready to leave in ten minutes. She not only needed to get out of the house, but she also needed to talk, and he was good at getting her to talk even if it took making her mad. In five minutes, she climbed up into his truck and they set out for the stock yard.

Richard waited until they turned out of their driveway before speaking. "Allie, I know something's bothering you." When she stared at him like he'd lost his mind, he added, "I mean beyond the fact you've lost your brother. Not leaving the farm, not wanting to see Luke or your other friends, that's not like you and it's not good for you. Can you please tell me what's wrong?"

Crying again, Allie turned to look out the window, trying to figure out how to say what she had been feeling. "I shouldn't have gone to meet Liz that morning. If I had just stayed home, I would have noticed Joey hadn't turned up for breakfast and gone to check on him sooner. He might still be alive if I'd just not gone to play a stupid game." There, she'd said it and meant it and she was sure no one would understand.

What her dad said next grabbed her full attention. "Oh, honey, that's not true! For Joey to be that ill when you found him, even if you'd gone there at two that morning, it would almost certainly have been too late. That's how fast acting and deadly COVID can be. I should know because I talked to Tommy and to the emergency room doctor who examined Joey that morning. There would have been nothing any of us could do."

"Why did you check with Tommy and the doctor?" was all she could think to say.

"Because your mom and I went through the same thing you're going through. We thought if we'd just not gone to the stock yard that morning then we could have saved Joey's life. That was one reason your mom wanted the two of us to go alone at the hospital to see Joey. We needed to get our thoughts straight before we could be of any help to you and Gil."

Allie was sobbing by the time Richard finished speaking. "You mean I really couldn't have made a difference if I'd found Joey sooner? Are you sure?"

"Yes, honey," he said, just as they pulled into the stock yard parking lot. Instead of driving around to the pick-up area, he parked and took her hand. "So please stop beating yourself up for something over which you had no control. Remember what your Bible study lessons have been teaching—

God has His plan and we don't always understand it, but we have to trust Him. Are you okay now? Will you promise me you'll absolve yourself from feeling guilty?"

Nodding, she promised and even smiled, realizing her heart felt lighter and her head clearer than it had since that awful day. Her dad was right. She needed to rejoin the land of the living one step at a time and that step would be to call Luke and invite him over for a long walk. She had missed him so much and needed him even more. Now that her head was clear, they had some catching up to do.

They picked up the calves and headed home, where they found Liz helping Rae with a project in the den. Richard said hello, grabbed a cup of coffee, and went in search of Gil to help him unload the cows. Allie joined the ladies, who were in the midst of picking out paint colors for the room. Rae had been talking about painting for a long time and it was obviously time, especially since she had some extra hands around for the next few days.

When the phone rang and Rae went to answer it, Liz was glad of the opportunity to talk with Allie alone. "It seems like forever since we just chatted about whatever's going on and I, for one, am ready to do just that. Want to go for a walk after lunch? I could do with the exercise and the temperature is just right for a stroll down to the big pond." She was happy when Allie agreed and even happier to notice her best friend seemed a bit brighter in spirit. It had been six days since Joey's death and she wanted to find a way to help Allie if she could.

Rae returned and they picked out the wall and trim colors before deciding it was time to fix lunch. Gil and Richard returned to the house around noon to find lunch about ready and the ladies arguing over which recipe was best for deviled eggs. It was wonderful to hear them animated over something so trivial and to hear their laughter as the debate carried over into lunchtime. Richard was reminded of the verse about a merry heart being good like medicine and his family having even a tiny bit of merriment was music to his ears.

Liz and Allie took their time walking through the fields to the pond, chatting about this and that, and enjoying the relaxed company of a good friend. Allie thought it was nice just getting out of her own head, which was thanks to the earlier talk with her dad. Luke would be by after dinner, and she was happy thinking about spending time with him.

Liz interrupted her reverie, "You know, Gil and I walked up here a couple of days ago and pretended to fish for a while before giving up and just sitting quietly until he shared something that had been bothering him. I'm wondering if that same something might be what's been weighing you down too."

Although a bit taken aback, Allie thought she might know what Liz was talking about and took her time before replying. "I didn't realize Gil was bothered by anything. He didn't mention it to me, but I'm glad he's comfortable enough with you to discuss it. What was bothering him?"

"He's been feeling guilty, thinking he might have been able to do something to save Joey's life. He thought maybe he'd missed some sign that Joey was ill or that he should have gone to Blessed Acres II first thing that morning, thinking he might have gotten help sooner and made a difference." Liz looked at Allie to see how she was accepting what she was saying. She didn't want to intrude or step on Allie's toes, but she also didn't want her friend to suffer with the same thoughts and emotions.

"You know, you're very intuitive. That's probably one reason why you're so good with kids. I have been struggling with the same thing, and it's about broken my heart. That's why I've been a bit remote, even with Luke and the family. But Dad called me out on it this morning and told me even he and mom had dealt with the guilt of thinking they should have done things differently that morning. He also explained that they had talked with Tommy and the ER doctor and were assured it wouldn't have made a difference if Joey had gotten help an hour or two hours sooner. How was Gil after your talk?" Allie was anxious to know if her oldest brother was still struggling and might need her help.

"He had talked with Tommy too, and that had helped a lot, but he just couldn't clear the feeling in his heart." Liz stopped to lower herself onto the bank of the pond before going on. "My only point of reference is how I felt after Chris died. My guilt almost suffocated me because I was the reason he went for a ride that day. He asked me to go for a ride with him, and I was adamant that he go alone so I could have time to get some silly chores done. If I'd gone with him, things might have turned out differently. We might have taken a different route, stopped for ice cream, or come home sooner for some reason. Who knows? Unfortunately, I didn't have family nearby to support me, and I didn't know God. In fact, I turned all my pent-up guilt and what-ifs into a sizzling anger toward God. Then, that day that I accepted Jesus as my Savior, all that anger evaporated. Allie, you've been teaching me to trust God and to believe He has a purpose and plan for me. He also had a plan for Joey."

Without thinking, Allie blurted out, "But he was so young and truly happy serving the Lord. Remember how he talked when we all went to Olaf's that night after Christmas? For a quiet man, it couldn't have been easy to open up and share his heart, but he did and with such joy."

Smiling at that precious memory, Liz answered, "That was precious and so much for Joey to share." When Allie nodded in agreement, Liz felt comfortable to go on. "Trusting God to work in our lives includes trusting His timing to be perfect according to His plan—not our timing or our plan but His. You know that! Who do you think taught me?" Now, they both were laughing and it felt wonderful, like opening a cage and allowing a bird its freedom for the first time in a long time.

They prayed together before starting back to the house. Life would never be quite the same, but it would be life according to the Master's plan and life remembering a sweet, young man who loved his family, his music, his wood working, but most of all his Lord.

Chapter 21

A week later quarantine at the Lambert farm was over and thankfully no one had gotten ill. Rae's painting squad had finished in the den and had even gotten halfway finished with the dining room, which she and Allie would finish over the next few days. Liz was busy with school committee meetings, and Gil and Richard were back to their usual farm schedule.

In mid-July, Pastor Harwell reinstated in-person worship services at Southside. That included Sunday morning and evening but not Sunday school. The sanctuary was open for everyone, and the fellowship hall was set up with a big screen for watching livestream for those who wished to attend but still practice social distancing and/or wear a mask. All areas of the church facility would receive a deep cleaning after the Sunday services, which prompted the decision to leave Wednesday night service livestream-only for a while.

Along with the decision to reopen the church, Cayden's working from home on a regular basis came to an end. Daniel didn't realize how much he'd come to rely on his wife for many things associated with his ministry and running the church until she was no longer at home most of the time and unavailable to help here and there. She had officially moved her church membership to Aylett Baptist after their wedding, but now he was thinking he might need her to do one more thing for him and he began praying for God's guidance.

Two days later, Daniel was ready to discuss his proposal with his lovely bride. "Sweetheart, I've got something to discuss with you. I need you to think about what I'm about to say and pray about it before you answer because it's a pretty big deal."

"I just knew something was up but I couldn't figure out what. I was pretty sure it's not something bad or I would have gotten it out of you sooner." Taking his hand, she asked, "So what's up?"

"First, I have to apologize and then thank you for all the church stuff you've helped me with since we got married. I mean, having you at home pretty much 24/7 has been wonderful, and having Cayden the super-secretary at my beck and call has been an absolute Godsend," he added with a grin.

"Well, thank you, kind sir. It's been my pleasure to help my husband in any way possible. You don't have to thank me for that, but I do appreciate the sweet words. Oh, yeah, you said 'first,' which must mean there's more. Hit me with it. I'm ready!" she said cheekily.

"Okay, here's the thing. Would you consider resigning as secretary at Southside and being my full-time secretary?" Seeing her surprised look, he hurried on, "The pay won't be quite as much but close, and the benefits would be better."

Pretending to consider his question, Cayden replied in a very businesslike manner. "Pastor Daniel, I thought you'd never ask!"

Sweeping her off her feet and kissing her face all over, Daniel couldn't contain his glee. "You're serious? You've thought about it and would like to work alongside me each day?"

"Well, first of all, I hope you don't treat all job candidates in such a manner. If so, I'll have to be sure to sit in on all interviews and employment offers going forward." They were both laughing by that point. "Of course, I would. Mrs. Dean does a great job as your part-time, unpaid secretary, but I know it ties up time she would be happy doing other things around their horse farm or with their family. I just didn't want to put the idea into your head, but I've been praying about it and obviously God has laid it on your heart. So there we have it. I can't possibly say no. Now, tell me about the better benefits."

Pastor Harwell wasn't surprised when Cayden handed in her official resignation the following day. Although he was sad to think of her leaving their office, he totally understood what a blessing she would be working side-by-side with Daniel. They came up with a plan where she would work from home two days a week and the other three in the office until they could find a replacement. That would allow her to continue assisting Daniel and take care of all her duties at Southside. Two weeks later, a new member of Southside, Joyce Porter, was hired and one week of training later Cayden officially left Southside's employ and became secretary at Aylett Baptist.

Simon and Coral still continued to hold out a very small hope that adoptions from China that had already been approved would go through as planned, although they couldn't see how with the world locked down. At first, they were sure the authorities would just postpone adoptions, but as time went by, it was obvious their plans to bring Bo home and raise him as their own little boy might not come to fruition. When the announcement came that China would no longer carry out intercountry adoptions, their hearts were once again broken, but not like last year when there seemed to be no hope. They continued to believe that God had a purpose even in something so shattering and that He would lead them as He'd done before according to His plan, His will, His timing.

Chapter 22

*A*llie, who stayed busy preparing lessons for the online teaching she would be doing in September, found her thoughts constantly straying to Luke, and a plan began to take shape in her mind. The past months had been a rude awakening to just how precious life is and that no one is promised tomorrow. After a quick phone call to Luke and a chat with her mom, she was ready to put her plan into action.

Luke came to the farm that evening expecting to join the Lamberts for dinner but found only Allie busily setting the table for only two. She stopped to give him a quick kiss before hurrying to pour tea. Thinking back over their time dating, he'd always seen her helping Rae in the kitchen but never actually cooking a meal, but he liked this new aspect of the amazing woman he was blessed to love.

"What's wrong, Luke?" she asked, stopping to tilt her head and look at him. "Why are you looking at me funny?"

"I'm just wondering who this beautiful young woman wearing an apron and scurrying around the kitchen is. Also, where's your mom and dad? You gotta admit this is unusual." He ended with a grin when she quickly pulled the apron off as if she'd not meant to still be wearing it when he arrived.

"Well, you're right. Mom does most of the cooking, but I do my fair share. You just haven't had the privilege of eating my cooking, but that's about to change. It occurred to me this morning that I've never cooked a meal for you, and this seemed like the perfect opportunity. So I hope you're ready for a simple yet tasty meal," she finished as she put the last dish on the table. "And, oh yeah, here's a tip for you—even if you're not ready for what I've fixed, pretend like you are!"

Of course, this had them laughing as they sat down, asked the blessing, and began to eat. A lot of their time over the last months had been rushed and their actions dictated by circumstances beyond their control. But she was determined tonight would be different. They would take their time enjoying blackened salmon, asparagus, and rice pilaf and talk about mundane things that had little or no consequence. The very idea of a relaxed, carefree evening with Luke made her heart sing.

"Last night, you said you were going to work on lesson plans today. Did you make much progress?" Allie asked while refilling their glasses.

Looking a bit sheepish, he filled her in on how his plan for the day had changed. "Well, to be honest, I didn't touch my lesson plans. Daniel called, said he had a free morning, and invited me to golf with him."

"Luke Carson, I bet that was one tough decision—lesson plans or golf with Daniel! And which did you choose, hmmm?" she teased. Laughing easily was such fun with him, especially when he made a sad, rather repentant face. "Don't try to fool me. I know what you decided and you're not one bit sad you did it, either. And neither am I. Now tell me all about how wonderfully you golfed."

Conversation continued through the end of their meal, and they decided to wait a while to have dessert. He could see a beautiful coconut layer cake on the counter but was just too full from the delicious dinner she'd prepared. When he suggested a walk, she agreed wholeheartedly.

As they walked along hand-in-hand in companionable silence, he realized yet another aspect of this woman that he loved—she didn't feel the need to talk all the time but was happy with quiet times. He was glad they were heading to the swings in the field by the big barn. He had some things to share with her and that would be the perfect spot.

However, Allie had plans of her own and suggested they keep walking. Unlike him, she had spent the entire morning working on lesson plans and was in need of a little exercise. As they continued, she decided it was time to share her heart.

"Luke, this year has been hard in so many ways, and I've learned one thing above all else. Life is meant to be lived. Each day should be treasured and lived to the fullest because no one knows if they even have another tomorrow. And time is a commodity we shouldn't squander." She stopped, looked him in the eyes, and simply stated, "Luke, I love you. I didn't want to waste another minute not telling you how I've been feeling for a while now."

His reaction was not quite what she'd imagined it would be. "Allie, you stole my thunder!"

Sputtering, she could only look at him for a second but then regained her voice. "What in the world do you mean, I stole your thunder? What thunder and how did I steal it? What an odd thing to say when your girlfriend gets up the nerve to open her heart. I never!" And she took off, walking quickly back toward the house.

Jogging to catch up with her, he gently took her arm and turned her toward him so that he could see her face. "I was planning to tell you that I love you this evening. Had it all planned out, in fact. We'd walk to the swings and I would tell the most wonderful woman in the world how blessed I am to have her in my life and that I love her with all my heart."

"Really?" As she spoke, her voice broke just a little. "You're not just saying that to smooth things over? Because you know I wouldn't want that."

Taking her in his arms, he looked deep into her eyes and said it the way he should have earlier. "Allie, I love you. I've known it for a while, but the timing just hasn't been right to tell you. But that's in the past and, like you said, we have today and we should live it to the fullest." He followed that declaration with a kiss and a promise to tell her that he loved her often.

"Oh, yeah, I have something else to share with you. Could we go to the swings now?" he asked like a very happy kid who'd just been given the keys to an ice cream truck. They ambled back through the field to the swings, filling in all the blanks about when they'd realized they loved each other and how much and who loved who the most.

As they enjoyed the gentle motion of the swings and the cooler evening breeze, Luke filled her in on something exciting that had happened to him a few days earlier. He'd needed time to decide what he thought of it before even bringing it up with Allie.

"You remember when I told you how much I'd like to teach history on the college level?" When she nodded, he went on, "Well, one of my college buddies teaches at a Bible college and put my name in the running for a history professor position that's only just opened up."

"Luke, that's fantastic! You'd be a wonderful history professor, and I truly believe teaching in a Bible college versus a secular college would be just the thing." Her enthusiasm was the key to opening up and letting her see how excited he was about the prospect.

"I agree. My buddy Matthew Scott teaches physical education and health and coaches men's basketball. He and his family love it there. The selection committee called me two days ago inviting me to come in for an interview, and I've been praying to know my heart before even bringing it up to you." Seeing she had questions, he stopped, allowing her time to speak.

"Where is the school? When would you start? Are they even having classes with the pandemic still a factor?" Her questions were all valid and showed she was truly thinking about what he was saying, but her next question was the most pointed. "And why would you even hesitate to bring it up with me?"

He answered each question in turn. "The school, Mountainvale College, is near Harrisonburg, Virginia. Remember when we went skiing? The college is about thirty minutes from there. I would start teaching online in November and then in the classroom beginning in January, when they plan to reopen for regular in-person classes. I didn't want to even bring it up if it wasn't something I was interested in pursuing."

"What?" she almost yelled. "Of course, you'd tell me about even being asked. But I hadn't thought that it might not be near Fredericksburg or Richmond. That wouldn't be a doable commute. Wow, so many questions are swirling in my mind!"

"Okay, so why I wanted to be sure is because I want to know something important from you before I can make the final decision. Just to be clear, I am not proposing." Before he could finish his statement, she interrupted.

"Proposing? First, you're telling me about a possible job offer and now we're talking about you proposing? I'm getting confused, but I must admit the word 'proposing' got my attention," she finished with wide eyes and a sweet grin.

"Allie, I love you and know that I want to spend the rest of my life with you. I also know you have told me several times about how you are a homebody and didn't really like even being away at Radford for college. So if that's how you really feel, I would not ask you to consider leaving here and moving two hours away. That's why I prefaced my other statement with 'I am not proposing.' A proposal should be romantic and special and certainly not just one factor to be considered in making a career decision." Although he'd squatted down in front of her as he talked, he still couldn't see her face because she was looking down at her feet. Gently lifting her chin, he asked, "Does that make sense?"

"Now I'll say 'just to be clear' because I need to make sure I understand. Are you saying you'll not ask me to move away if I prefer not to but you'll still go without me? Or are you saying you wouldn't take the position if I didn't want to leave home?" She looked directly and calmly into his eyes waiting for his answer, because it was a very important answer.

"Let me make this very clear because I seem to be having a problem being succinct. I would like to accept the position but will only do so if you, my love, are willing to marry me and move with me." He finished his statement just as she jumped off the swing and almost knocked him over.

"Let me be just as clear. Call them first thing tomorrow morning and arrange the interview. I'll marry you whenever you like and be happy to go with you wherever you like, just as long as we're together!" She launched herself into his arms as soon as he could get to his feet and cried happy tears of joy and relief on his shoulder.

Chapter 23

So much had been happening, and it was hard dealing with it without their usual support group of friends, which to Cayden and Daniel meant it was time to invite the gang over for a potluck dinner if everyone felt comfortable getting together. Ila, Wyatt, and Phillip were in North Carolina visiting with his family, but everyone else agreed they would enjoy a relaxed time with friends. Simon and Coral were first to arrive, followed quickly by Allie, Luke, Liz, Gil, Brandon, and Faith. When all their food offerings were set out and they were ready to eat, Daniel asked them to join hands as he prayed.

"Dear Lord, thank you most of all for loving us and your many blessings on us. I thank you for each person here and what they mean to Cayden and me. You've brought us through some hard times lately, and we thank you for your loving arms holding us and giving us strength and comfort. Lord, we thank you for this wonderful food and the hands that prepared it. Please bless it and use it to strengthen our bodies. Lord, use us to further your kingdom. We ask this all in Jesus's name. Amen." Daniel heard several "Amens" echo around the room and then one loud "Let's eat!" from Brandon. And eat they did!

No activities or games were planned for the evening. It was just a time of sweet communion and was sorely needed. Burdens as well as joys were shared. Cayden found herself keeping an eye on Allie, but she found Luke more than up to the task of making sure her precious friend was okay. She then noticed how the seating placed Gil and Liz together and neither of them seemed to mind. In fact, they were happy chatting and laughing, which was music to Cayden's ears. Also, it was obvious to her that Brandon and Faith's relationship was deepening, and she thanked the Lord her old friend had found a special someone. Simon and Coral just appeared to be taking it all in, enjoying a time to put cares aside for the evening.

Cayden thought back over the last year and its joys and sorrows for her, Daniel, and their friends. There were so many times God's hand was evident, and she could easily discern His plan. While at other times, she just had to simply trust that He was working according to His plan and His timing. As Daniel walked up and took her in his arms, she whispered, "God is good all the time and all the time God is good!"

And just as she finished speaking, Luke stood and said, "Allie and I have an announcement to make."

About Kharis Publishing

Kharis Publishing, an imprint of Kharis Media LLC, is a leading Christian and inspirational book publisher based in Aurora, Chicago metropolitan area, Illinois. Kharis' dual mission is to give voice to under-represented writers (including women and first-time authors) and equip orphans in developing countries with literacy tools. That is why, for each book sold, the publisher channels some of the proceeds into providing books and computers for orphanages in developing countries so that these kids may learn to read, dream, and grow. For a limited time, Kharis Publishing is accepting unsolicited queries for nonfiction (Christian, self-help, memoirs, business, health and wellness) from qualified leaders, professionals, pastors, and ministers. Learn more at: https://kharispublishing.com/

www.ingramcontent.com/pod-product-compliance
Lightning Source LLC
Chambersburg PA
CBHW051424090426
42737CB00014B/2811